All Aboard for Santa Fe

All Aboard for Santa Fe

**Railway Promotion
of the Southwest,
1890s to 1930s**

VICTORIA E. DYE

University of New Mexico Press
Albuquerque

11 10 09 08 07 06 05   1 2 3 4 5 6 7

Library of Congress Cataloging-in-Publication Data

Dye, Victoria E., 1959–
  All aboard for Santa Fe : railway promotion of the Southwest,
1890s to 1930s / Victoria E. Dye.
      p. cm.
  Includes bibliographical references and index.
  ISBN 0-8263-3657-4 (cloth : alk. paper)
  1. Railroad travel—New Mexico—Santa Fe—Marketing—History.
  2. Atchison, Topeka, and Santa Fe Railroad Company—History.
  3. City promotion—New Mexico—Santa Fe—History. 4. Tourism—
New Mexico—Santa Fe—History. 5. Santa Fe (N.M.)—History.
I. Title.
  HE2781.S46D94 2005
  385'.06'5789509—dc22

                                            2005008741

Book design and composition by Damien Shay
Body type is Adobe Garamond 11/14.
Display is Tiger Rag and Railroad Gothic.

Para Doug

CONTENTS

LIST OF ILLUSTRATIONS

ACKNOWLEDGMENTS

This book is based on research that developed from my interests in tourism and New Mexico history, which came together in a study of the various marketing strategies used by the Atchison, Topeka, and Santa Fe Railroad to showcase Santa Fe, New Mexico, as a southwestern travel destination. The work emphasizes a sixty-year period from 1880, when the rails were laid through New Mexico, through World War II (the early 1940s). This is followed by a brief treatment of railroad advertisements through the 1950s as they pertained to selling Santa Fe, and an assessment of relevant contemporary advertising and statistics by city and state tourism departments. I have chosen to be selective rather than inclusive due to difficulties in acquiring rare promotional materials. This work is not about individuals, civic groups, or the cultures of Santa Fe and the Southwest; rather, this work focuses on how the Atchison, Topeka, and Santa Fe Railroad systems wanted Santa Fe to be seen by outsiders. My objective was to analyze how the railroad used the cultural and scenic highlights of Santa Fe and its environs to their advantage in marketing the area as a travel destination; because of these progressive strategies, the town of Santa Fe continues to be a popular vacation spot.

In the process of researching this work I have relied on many people who have helped me to see this project reach fruition. This book would not be complete without acknowledging those who made it possible. Several resources and archivists were instrumental in assisting me in my efforts to dig up pertinent information regarding my research. Deb Slaney from the Albuquerque Museum; Kathleen Ferris, Nancy Brown, and Mary Alice Tsosie from the Center for Southwest Research; Laree Dates from the Heard Museum; and Brian Graney from the New Mexico State Records Center and Archives all helped me to find sources under their care. Special thanks are due to Tomas Jaehan and Diane Block from the Museum of New Mexico, and to Connie Menninger and Nancy Sherbert with the Kansas State Historical Society in Topeka for their interest in the subject and for tracking down difficult-to-find brochures. Lisa Bertelli and the folks at the La Fonda were helpful in securing photographs. Additionally, Suzanne Burris and Patrick Hiatte were instrumental in helping me to obtain copyright permission for many promotional items such as the Burlington Northern and Santa Fe Railway Company, the Atchison, Topeka, and Santa Fe Railway logo, and associated images that are registered trademarks of the Burlington Northern and Santa Fe Railway Company, and are used here with permission © 2004 The Burlington and Santa Fe Railway Company. Thanks to all of you for your help and suggestions.

Deserving special mention are those who read several drafts of the initial manuscript and made valuable comments on contents and format. I am indebted to Professor Joseph Pitti in the History Department at California State University, Sacramento, for his expertise and his interest in my original thesis, and his continued support in seeing it published. His wonderful sense of humor, and our common roots in New Mexico, made this a memorable project. I would also like to thank Professor Christopher Castaneda from the History Department at California State University, Sacramento, for his patience, critical comments, and suggestions.

Several words of recognition are in order for those who were gracious enough to give me their time and offered suggestions and insight into this project. These include Mary Kay Cline from the Albuquerque Convention and Visitors Bureau, Carol Garcia from the New Mexico Department of Tourism, and Southwestern historian Cheryl J. Foote, who helped me with information regarding New Mexico cuisine. I am particularly grateful to historian Marc Simmons for his generosity and his insights into the history of this region.

I am deeply indebted to the many people who labored over the exhausting job of reading and rereading through these pages. These include Dr. Joseph Pitti (who read it several times and proofed my

ACKNOWLEDGMENTS

additions), Ann Kelt, Douglas Kelt, Joleene Kobetich, Michelle Snapp, and Dirk Van Vuren; thank you all for your corrections and suggestions. Sincere appreciation goes to Damien Shay and Maya Allen-Gallegos from the University of New Mexico Press for their help throughout the process. I wish to give special recognition to Joleene Kobetich, for her assistance with research in several archives across the country, as well as for her time, support, and her delightful company.

Finally, to those who helped with words of encouragement and support and have on several occasions shared with me the amazing blue skies of New Mexico and the rich beauty of the landscape below them. These include Bisti, Brenda and Clarence Dye, Gail and McSene Kobetich, Joleene Kobetich, Jennifer Elderidge Jeffries, Michelle, Robert, and Jamie Snapp, William (Butter) Tafoya, and the special group of people (Techies) I have maintained strong ties with, from over twenty years ago, while living in Socorro, and who have inquired about my progress on this project along the way. Additionally, special appreciation goes to Douglas Kelt, for his continued support and patience, and for encouraging me to get this work published.

INTRODUCTION

B y the late 1800s the main mode of transportation for travelers to the Southwest was by railroad. In 1878, the Atchison, Topeka, and Santa Fe Railway Company (AT&SF) became the first railroad to enter New Mexico, and by the late 1890s it controlled over half of all of the track miles in the Territory.[1] The company wielded tremendous power in New Mexico, and it applied this power to make tourism an important financial enterprise. The AT&SF was not the only railroad system to promote destinations to tourists. Before the Santa Fe Railroad was selling the Southwest, the Southern Pacific promoted its own Hotel Del Monte in Monterey, California, which opened in 1880. Seventeen years later they enhanced this by adding the first golf course west of the Mississippi, and by 1919 they were promoting the Pebble Beach resort area, also in Monterey. In the early 1900s, the Canadian Pacific was marketing its great northern route through the scenic canyons of the Rocky Mountains to prospective settlers and tourists. To foster passenger travel in the Southwest, the AT&SF became the first industry to exploit its captivating history and alluring attractions and to advertise Santa Fe as the essence of the Southwest.[2]

Connected in 1880 by an eighteen-mile railroad spur from the town of Lamy, Santa Fe became a popular destination where tourists could see the unchanging reminders of ancient native cultures that flourished in the area. Between 1880 and 1940, Santa Fe changed from a "sleepy" Southwest town to a flourishing tourist mecca, largely through the marketing efforts of the railroad. Consequently, a visitor to Santa Fe in 1930

1

would have experienced a very different town than a visitor only fifteen or twenty years earlier. The city's transformations included changes in perception as well as material changes in the lives of the people who lived in and around Santa Fe.

Several works have investigated particular components of this transformation, yet none are specific to Santa Fe and its emergence as a visitor destination. Two studies discussed how the railroad promoted Native Americans as a Southwestern attraction.[3] Leah Dilworth provided a detailed study of the different promotional campaigns in the Southwest and how they portrayed the Indians in Arizona and New Mexico, and D. H. Thomas wrote about the Indian Detour sightseeing company established by the AT&SF and Fred Harvey.[4] Thomas traced the beginning of the company and its promotional efforts, the training of the "dudes" and couriers, and the routes of the tours through the Indian country in New Mexico and Arizona. Other books of interest include Chris Wilson's *The Myth of Santa Fe* and Peter Hertzog's *La Fonda*.[5] These works, however, only briefly address the purpose of the present study, which is to investigate how and by what means the AT&SF promoted Santa Fe, New Mexico, from 1880 to the beginning of World War II, and to what extent this effort was successful. In its promotional efforts, the AT&SF joined forces with other entities, including the Fred Harvey Company, the Bureau of Immigration, and the Santa Fe Chamber of Commerce.

To analyze various concepts and strategies used by the railroad company to establish Santa Fe as a traveler's destination, this study relies mainly on the numerous promotional materials that the railroad used to acquaint visitors with regional culture, the area's history, and its cultural diversity, especially that of the native Indians. This inquiry is not intended to provide a complete history of the Santa Fe Railroad, the Fred Harvey Company, or the capital city of Santa Fe, as numerous works already address these topics.[6] Rather, this study provides insights concerning the origins and maintenance of the "Santa Fe Mystique" that continues to draw tourists from across the country and around the world. Developing this mystique was an intentional marketing strategy of the Atchison, Topeka, and Santa Fe Railroad, and is largely responsible for putting this Southwestern town on the map, even though the main line was eighteen miles to the south.

INTRODUCTION

To provide historical context, I begin with a synoptic outline of the history of Santa Fe. The AT&SF cleverly incorporated and embellished this extraordinary history in its promotional materials, and it became an important component of the railroad's advertising campaign. It is also important to understand the origins of the Santa Fe Railroad and its competition with other railways to gain access to the New Mexico Territory and to Santa Fe. Railroad companies competed for land, buying large tracts and securing property for right-of-way, and later reselling or leasing these properties for a profit. The purchases and leases of railroad property also provided settlers with the opportunity to move west and begin a new life.[7]

Medical doctors in the late 1880s believed that the dry, clean air of the Southwest was a cure for tuberculosis, and that Santa Fe offered a perfect location for patients to recuperate. The railroad capitalized on this belief to sell the Santa Fe area as a destination for health seekers. Another campaign carried out by the Santa Fe Railroad before the 1920s included the sale of railroad land. During this time, the firm encouraged the purchase of fertile lands, both its own and that of other real estate dealers, by using railroad brochures to highlight the success of farming and ranching on these lands, thereby promoting passenger-ticket sales to Santa Fe. These efforts to sell Santa Fe are the focus of chapter 2.

Probably the most significant and effective campaign to promote Santa Fe involved the combined marketing efforts of the Santa Fe Railroad and the Fred Harvey Company. They developed promotional materials emphasizing the Indian and Hispanic cultures, involving talented artists from the Santa Fe art colony and the Indian Detours sightseeing guides, which left an impression in the minds of travelers of what could be seen and experienced in Santa Fe. This impression was so significant that Santa Fe continues to capitalize on art and culture to attract tourists to this day. This historic collaboration is the subject of chapter 3.

Chapter 4 examines events and ongoing attractions that the Santa Fe helped to promote in many of its brochures. The most important of these was the Santa Fe Fiesta, which showcased the distinct ethnic groups from the area and continues to attract tourists from all over the world. Other cultural features were the unique cuisine and the intriguing architectural style. Many of the Santa Fe Railroad's brochures highlighted the unique Pueblo and Spanish architecture, and pictures of old missions and adobe buildings frequently dominated the covers of its brochures. The ongoing success of the Santa Fe tourism industry underscores the success of the marketing efforts of the Atchison, Topeka, and Santa Fe Railroad, and may be seen as testimony to the unprecedented use of regional motifs and cultural icons in marketing and tourism throughout the twentieth century.

While Santa Fe became synonymous with the Southwestern regional motif, Albuquerque struggled to gain recognition as a southwestern tourist destination. However, New Mexico's largest metropolitan area came into its own as a commercial center in large part due to the development of the railroad, and areas of the town have maintained a degree of historic preservation as discussed in chapter 5. The concluding chapter gives highlights of the railroad's massive campaign that successfully promoted its namesake town, a town not even on the railroad's mainline, and the means by which the town continues to maintain its dominance as a tourism destination.

HISTORY OF SANTA FE AND THE SANTA FE RAILWAY SYSTEM

Santa Fe

Notrh America's first capital city, Santa Fe, has enticed travelers for generations with its Pueblo-style architecture and deep-rooted heritage. Visitors have traveled to Santa Fe for hundreds of years to trade, visit, or live amid the enchanting landscape. Over the last century the city has become synonymous with Southwestern culture, arts and crafts, cuisine, and architecture. The history of Santa Fe has spanned centuries, beginning long before the Spaniards laid claim to the territory; various Southwestern cultures traded with one another, and both before and after the Spanish conquest the people living in the area mixed with one another, creating a distinct Hispanic culture. In spite of the fusing of ethnicities, the Pueblo maintained their identity and a degree of sovereignty. Lured to Santa Fe by the spectacular beauty of this region, visitors had the opportunity to travel by rail on the AT&SF and experience the unique cultural heritage and rich history of this ancient city.

Officials of the Santa Fe Railway Company were aware of the extraordinary history of ancient Southwestern cultures. The railroad realized that it could generate revenue by promoting this history, thereby stimulating growth in tourism.[1] The city of Santa Fe, occupied for over fourteen hundred years and the oldest state capital in the United States, had a colorful history indeed. Pueblo Indians, with a distinct culture and an economy well suited to their needs, were the initial inhabitants of the area. They and the Casas Grandes peoples from Chihuahua traded with the Durango and Zacatec cultures of Mexico via the *Camino Real de Tierra Adentro* (Inland Royal Highway), an ancient roadway that followed the foothills of Mexico's Sierra Madre Occidental. Via this interior trail, used as far back as 1000 A.D., Pueblo peoples received goods from as far as Central America such as marine shells, and parrots and macaws and their feathers, in exchange for turquoise, pottery, salt, and bison parts.[2] Centuries later iron tracks would follow this route, aiding trade by a faster mode of transportation.

Spaniards began to use the ancient trail for their slave raids as early as 1530.[3] Only ten years later, Coronado and his expedition marched over this route into New Mexico. The Camino Real subsequently became the primary route of communication from Mexico City to the northern part of New Spain and the means by which the arid regions were occupied and added to the Spanish Empire. By 1580, this road extended 850 miles north to present-day Chihuahua. Consequently, it was also known as the Chihuahua Trail and more than two centuries later it would continue to be a major trade route to the United States— an extension of the Santa Fe Trail.

Later in the 1500s, an additional route extended this ancient roadway. The route did not follow the Rio Grande as the trail of the native people did, but lay overland east of the river. Founded in 1598 by Governor Don Juan de Oñate, this new route lengthened the trail by seven hundred miles into the area of what is now New Mexico. This segment of the road was referred to by some as the Rio Grande Pueblo Trail. Oñate, whose mission was to "pacify the Pueblo and colonize New Mexico," extended the trail as far north as San Gabriel, which became New Mexico's first capital under the governor and his sergeant major, Vicente Zaldívar.[4]

A thirteen-hundred-mile trek over desert, the route from Mexico City to Santa Fe meandered between lava flows, across sand dunes, and through areas with only seasonally available water. Oñate and his colonists did not blaze this trail; they simply followed the footsteps of the many native people who had walked this route before Spanish explorers and emigrants first ventured into this new frontier. The

History of Santa Fe and the Santa Fe Railway System

Camino Real, the first Native American trail used by European emigrants and visitors in what is today the United States, represented the longest trade route in North America and a significant trail for the settlement of the Southwest.[5] Travelers from Chihuahua trekked over 350 miles before they crossed the Rio Grande at a site now called Oñate's Crossing, adjacent to present-day El Paso. The trail continued for over another three hundred miles to San Juan Pueblo, where Oñate established the settlement of San Gabriel. A few years later, in 1609, Don Pedro de Peralta moved the small colony of San Gabriel to the newly founded town of *La Ciudad de Santa Fe de San Francisco* (City of the Holy Faith of St. Francis), which then became the trail's terminus. The name of the town was subsequently abbreviated to Santa Fe.

Starting with Oñate, Spaniards frequently brutalized the natives along the Camino Real. During his first year of colonizing, Oñate's nephew, Juan de Zaldívar, was killed by a group of men from Ácoma "in retribution for attempting to gain provisions by force."[6] Oñate retaliated in January of 1599. With Spanish soldiers and Juan's younger brother, Oñate rode to Ácoma and killed eight hundred Pueblo people; he then took the survivors to San Gabriel where they were convicted of treason. Those prisoners younger than twelve were given to the Franciscan Mission (sixty girls were sent to Mexican convents), whereas those between the ages of twelve and twenty-five were made slaves. All of the men over twenty-five years of age had their right foot cut off.[7] The two Hopi who were visiting at the time were sent back to their village without their right hands.

Much of the conflict between Pueblo and Spanish likely was rooted in cultural ignorance. Although eight Pueblo communities existed around Santa Fe, each spoke a different dialect of the Tanoan linguistic family.[8] And whereas religious beliefs varied little from pueblo to pueblo, they differed profoundly from the Catholicism of the encroaching Spaniards, who "attempt[ed] to impose a strange and unwanted religion upon the native people [creating] the greatest source of conflict..."[9] Charles Lummis, the noted writer and booster of the ancient capital, claimed in 1923 that "no other town [in the United States] has a war record so bloody or a tenth so long" as Santa Fe.[10]

Founded in 1609, under the governorship of Pedro de Peralta, Santa Fe was built by the Spanish, literally and figuratively on the ruins of the

Pueblos. The new community became the capital of Spain's northern frontier in 1610, subsequently serving as the administrative and military center of Spain's northern frontier for almost two and a half centuries.

Spaniards exposed the Pueblos to new diseases, commandeered the Indians' food supplies, forced an unwanted religion upon them, interrupted established networks of trade with other tribes, and provoked an increasing number of raids by Apaches and Navajos. In the late 1670s, in response to the many Spanish injustices, Pueblos united in a secret revolt.[11] In August 1680 the Pueblo Indians rose up and "laid waste to Santa Fe," slaying Spaniards and driving the colonists from the territory.[12] For twelve years the capital city fell once again under the control of the Pueblos, but by 1692 it had been reclaimed under the authority of Governor Diego de Vargas.[13] Following some resistance, De Vargas captured the city and led efforts to rebuild the capital.

After Mexico gained independence from Spain in 1821, Santa Fe remained the capital city of Mexico's northern territory. The isolation of the town made its residents resistant to central control, and they enjoyed a certain degree of local autonomy; yet, as in most frontier societies, they had a need for goods that they were unable to manufacture. By this time Santa Feans began trading with foreigners to supplement the infrequent wagon trains from central Mexico. The caravans from Mexico City were expected to deliver supplies to Santa Fe annually, but turmoil and corruption within the Mexican government rendered the supply-train operations unreliable.[14] Additionally, Indian raids along the Camino Real delayed the caravans.[15] By 1824, trade extended from Missouri to Chihuahua, bringing goods from across the Great Plains to Santa Fe and then down the Camino Real. In the 1830s small revolts broke out against the central government, largely because the administration in Mexico City enforced church attendance and admonished settlers that they were not allowed to have slaves. These new rules that emanated from a distant and meddlesome government agitated many of the Mexican colonists in Santa Fe, and they began to trade more with the Americans. At the same time, New Mexico received more goods from the United States via the Santa Fe Trail than it did from Mexico by way of the Camino Real. Not only did the new commercial network bring merchandise to people hungry for manufactured goods, but the trade caravans from Missouri brought new ethnic groups and values to

History of Santa Fe and the Santa Fe Railway System

Santa Fe, all of which contributed to the community's rich and dynamic history.[16] At times these groups came into conflict with each other.

Cultural and political differences sparked the 1837 rebellion of Rio Arriba. In 1835, Santa Fean animosity toward the Mexican government reached a high point with the appointment of Albino Pérez as governor of New Mexico. Although Mexican officials imposed taxes, they supplied neither services nor military support.[17] Moreover, the new governor made no efforts to conceal either his luxurious lifestyle or his Santa Fe mistress (his wife remained in Mexico).[18] Angry both at forced taxation and their governor's profligate extravagances, rebels—consisting of Pueblos and northern New Mexicans—determined to set aside the new Mexican constitution and establish a democratic government.[19] Pérez and his troops marched out against the insurgents only to find themselves surrounded by rebel forces near the pueblo of San Ildefonso, south of Santa Fe. When negotiations with the rebels failed, the insurgents killed Pérez and seventeen civil and military officers in the subsequent scrimmage.[20] The rebels carried their prize—Pérez's decapitated head— on a pole to their camp in Santa Fe.

Despite their triumph over an apathetic and unsympathetic government in Mexico City, citizens of Santa Fe and the adjoining Pueblos soon found themselves under another regime. On August 15, 1846, General Stephen W. Kearny rode into Santa Fe and claimed New Mexico for the United States. Kearny's conquest of Santa Fe, part of the United States' campaign against Mexico during the Mexican-American War, was a bloodless affair, and within weeks he had gained the loyalty of many Pueblo leaders, established codes that recognized Mexican civil laws, and selected a site for Fort Marcy on a hill above the plaza of Santa Fe.[21] More than a year later, the 1847 Taos massacre claimed the life of the territory's first governor, Charles Bent, when Mexican soldiers and some northern Pueblo people conspired to oust the Anglo invaders from New Mexico. Colonel Sterling Price learned of the plot from Santa Fe's famous brothel owner, Gertrudes Barcelo. To avert an uprising, Price arrested several participants, but failed to apprehend the ringleader.[22] On January 19, 1847, a group of these conspirators attacked Taos, where they killed Sheriff Stephan Lee and Governor Bent. Although rebels also killed eight other Anglo-Americans north of Taos, over four hundred rebels subsequently lost their lives at a pitched battle near La Cañada.[23] Under orders from the United States Army, six of the conspirators were hanged and order was finally established by February 1847.[24]

The Treaty of Guadalupe Hidalgo, signed in 1848, made New Mexico a territory of the United States.[25] Santa Fe remained the capital city, but now fell under American rule. The violent rebellion at Rio Arriba and the Taos massacre were the last major revolts to affect Santa Feans. The bloody conflicts in New Mexico's past, especially the Pueblo Revolt of 1680, later became components that inspired Santa Fe folklore, dance, song, and even fiestas, as discussed in chapter 4. New Mexico's rich and colorful history of cultural conflict enticed writers, historians, and visitors alike.

The violence of the American Civil War a dozen years later never touched Santa Fe's Fort Marcy. But Santa Fe merchants, who purchased commodities brought over the Santa Fe Trail, supplied the quartermasters who rode between Fort Craig, south of Socorro, and Fort Union, northeast of Santa Fe. After the Confederate victory at the Battle of Valverde, across the river from Fort Craig, the Rebel forces were defeated at Glorieta Pass, twenty miles northeast of Santa Fe. Union forces won the Civil War in New Mexico at the Battle at Glorieta Pass, referred to as the "Gettysburg of the West."[26]

In the late 1870s the "Iron Horse" climbed over Glorieta Pass along the Santa Fe Trail northeast of Santa Fe and on through the Southwest, considerably facilitating the movement of passengers and cargo from Missouri to New Mexico. The merchants in Santa Fe anxiously looked forward to the railroad as a means to increase business and add to the population of their city. Nevertheless, because of the difficult terrain, the railroad bypassed Santa Fe in favor of a more direct route between Las Vegas and Albuquerque.[27] Disappointed but wanting not to miss out on the opportunity, the citizens of Santa Fe funded an 18.1-mile spur to connect Santa Fe to the line that ran southeast of the capital city.[28] When the railroad reached Santa Fe on February 9, 1880, traditional commerce over the Santa Fe Trail ended.[29] This mode of long-distance transportation shifted to the railway, and Santa Fe was suitably located between Chicago and Los Angeles. What had once been a long and dangerous journey over the dusty Santa Fe Trail soon became relatively routine and increasingly comfortable with the introduction of luxurious Pullman Palace sleeping cars. The first railroad to gain access to New Mexico and nationally promote the rich history and breathtaking beauty that surrounded the capital city was the

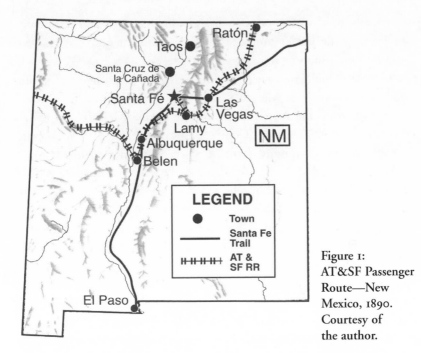

Figure 1:
AT&SF Passenger
Route—New
Mexico, 1890.
Courtesy of
the author.

Atchison, Topeka, and Santa Fe Railroad. Even though the main line never led to Santa Fe, the railroad sold Santa Fe as a major tourist destination, thereby increasing the number of passengers and commodities traveling along the AT&SF-owned tracks.

The Santa Fe Railway System

In 1859, Colonel Cyrus K. Holliday gained charter to the Atchison, Topeka, and Santa Fe Railroad (AT&SF), which provided for the issuance of one and one-half million dollars of stock in one-hundred-dollar shares and allowed the amount of stock to increase, but not to exceed the actual amount spent on the railway. Initially, land grants through Kansas and Texas were approved by Congress, which ruled that all railways had to be completed within ten years after Congress gave permission to commence construction. Failure to comply would mean that the railway company would lose its allotted federal lands. By 1864 congressional legislation had passed allowing the railroad to proceed into Colorado, which was accomplished in 1872.[30] As the AT&SF built westward, supply centers prospered, and construction workers brought families to settle lands along the railways. Construction of tracks to Santa Fe would soon be under way.

In 1874, Chief Engineer A. A. Robinson examined new and more direct routes into New Mexico from Dodge City, Kansas. Because of the long distance, the source of coal for the locomotives was an important consideration. Trinidad, Colorado, located in the eastern portion of the Rocky Mountains, offered such extensive coalfields that Robinson decided that the high cost of laying rail over the Rocky Mountains could be offset by the rich deposits.[31] Also concerned with the high cost of construction, the AT&SF's board of directors realized that the value of the wagon-borne merchandise moving down the Santa Fe Trail was estimated at over two million dollars annually, and that the same quantity of cargo could be moved by rail each week.[32] The promise of lucrative returns warranted construction into New Mexico as did the possibility of laying track all the way to the Pacific Coast, where other opportunities beckoned.[33]

Because of potential competition with the Southern Pacific Railroad Company, which had also been granted a charter to build through New Mexico, the AT&SF was determined to keep it and other railroads out of the state.[34] The main challenge came from the Denver and Rio Grande narrow-gauge railroad, which battled with the AT&SF for the right-of-way over the Colorado border into New Mexico.[35]

In 1878 the New Mexico legislature passed bills requiring the AT&SF to issue capital stock in the corporation for at least one thousand dollars for each mile of track to be laid in the territory, with at least 10 percent of the stock to be paid to the corporation before the AT&SF could be incorporated in New Mexico.[36] Meeting in 1879 to consider their options, AT&SF and New Mexico officials convened at the Exchange Hotel in Santa Fe. After a detailed investigation of the laws of incorporation, they discovered that the new regulations had not yet gone into effect. The executive committee made up of representatives from the Southern Pacific, New Mexico Southern Pacific, and the AT&SF railroads then incorporated under the name of the AT&SF.[37] This company became known simply as "the Santa Fe." Now the race was on. Making tracks through southeastern Colorado toward Raton Pass, New Mexico, the Denver and Rio Grande struggled to gain territory to claim right-of-way.

Figure 2: Lamy Junction, 1884. Photograph by J. R. Riddle. Courtesy of the Museum of New Mexico, neg. no. 76033.

The AT&SF arrived first, reaching New Mexico soil in November of 1878.[38] Once the right-of-way over Raton Pass had been secured, the AT&SF began to build a grade and to drill a 2,011-foot tunnel through the summit of the pass.[39] The railway engineers initially planned to construct tracks from Raton through Las Vegas to Santa Fe and on to Albuquerque, but unpredictable streams and rivers made construction difficult. The track eventually followed the Pecos River to the watershed of the Rio Grande and bypassed Santa Fe altogether. The closest the railroad got to Santa Fe was Galisteo Junction, renamed Lamy in 1881. Here the tracks were just over eighteen miles from the capital city. With urging from other Santa Fe officers and directors, the general manager of the Santa Fe Railroad, William Barstow Strong, accepted a proposal for a spur to be laid from Lamy to the capital.

Unfortunately, the AT&SF neglected to budget for this linkup.[40] Residents of Santa Fe and the surrounding area were upset at being bypassed, and they soon organized a committee to discuss means to fund a track from Santa Fe to the main line. Santa Fe officials offered the people of the capital city three alternatives. The first required Santa Fe County to give $175,000 in thirty-year, 7 percent bonds to the AT&SF, which would then build and operate the branch. The second option permitted

Santa Fe County to build its own track line, which would need to pass inspection for safety requirements by the chief engineers of the AT&SF. In the third option, Santa Fe County would both build and run its own railroad. The citizens chose the first alternative, to have the Santa Fe Railroad build and run the line, but they capped their contribution at $150,000 in bonds.[41] The AT&SF accepted the reduced amount, and by February 1878 the company had filed the papers for incorporation, and work began soon thereafter. Two years later, Governor Lew Wallace helped to drive the last spike. According to the *Weekly New Mexican*, the first locomotive arrived "amid a wild celebration."[42] This marked a turning point for the city that had three hotels and a population of 6,185.[43] In the following 114 years, Santa Fe would eventually grow to have over twenty-eight quality hotels, and a population of over 68,000,[44] becoming a destination for thousands of tourists seeking to experience this historic town and encounter what they often perceived as the unchanging cultural lifestyle of the area's native peoples.[45] Visitors could visit the local Pueblos or observe Indians decorated in their native attire selling their wares on the portal of the Palace of the Governors.[46] The AT&SF truly opened the gates for the capitalization of this cultural mecca.

In 1895, in the midst of an economic nationwide depression, the company went bankrupt and interested parties and bondholders took over the company's assets. Renamed the Atchison, Topeka, and Santa Fe Railway System, it continued to be known as "the Santa Fe."

To increase business for the railroad, the Santa Fe constantly sought new opportunities. In cooperation with territorial officials in the town of Santa Fe, the railroad company provided half-price rates to people attending the first Territorial Fair in 1881, and it distributed thousands of copies of *Territorial Bureau of Immigration*, which promoted land development in the area.[47] By 1903, Governor Miguel A. Otero reported that the AT&SF was "fostering industries and encouraging immigration along its lines. The . . . scenic and historic attraction reached by this line mean an ever increasing revenue for the railroad and the territory."[48] In years to follow, the railroad would use the climate, scenery, culture, and history of a town eighteen miles off the main line to generate income for its company.[49]

Chapter Two

HOW THE AT&SF MARKETED SANTA FE INTO THE EARLY 1920S

Funding the Santa Fe Railway's massive expansion through the Southwest required increased revenue. To generate ticket sales, the railroad used a variety of approaches to promote the majesty of the Southwest while emphasizing Santa Fe. These included highly competitive marketing, in which the railroad promoted the health benefits of the region as well as real estate and land opportunities. Additionally, it incorporated emblems that typified the Southwest, as well as the writings of literary icons, to sell the region to travelers.

These marketing approaches are presented in two segments. The first deals with marketing and advertising efforts prior to the Great Depression; the second focuses on the AT&SF, particularly the successful campaign called Indian Detours starting in the late 1920s and extending into the 1930s.

Competitive Marketing

The railroad's primary function initially was to ship freight and transport business travelers. After 1869, leisure travelers embraced train travel as a faster, safer, and more comfortable mode of transportation than overland stagecoach. To encourage passenger travel, the AT&SF created its own niche in the Southwest by promoting the culture, scenery, healthy climate, and fertile river valleys to be found in and around Santa Fe.

To challenge the Southern Pacific's monopoly, the AT&SF became the first industry to exploit the history and scenic attractions of New Mexico, and the town of Santa Fe represented the essence of the Southwest. While the Santa Fe Railroad laid tracks into New Mexico, the Southern Pacific Railroad opened its first western tourist resort in Monterey Bay to accommodate passengers and promote passenger travel to California.[1] This resort, called the Hotel del Monte, opened in 1880.

After enduring entrepreneurial conflicts, price wars, and competition from other companies for territory, the AT&SF needed additional revenue to offset expansion costs. This extra income funded the construction of rail lines to the Southwest and the Pacific Coast and compensated for overhead expenses. Starting in the 1880s, the AT&SF began its promotional campaign to sell Santa Fe as a travel destination. Company officers recognized the public's growing interest in the unique landscape of the arid Southwest, and they cleverly presented information for potential health seekers, settlers, and tourists.[2] With the end of the Civil War, tourism in the West began to pick up momentum, and provided many people from the eastern United States with a diversion from urbanization and industrialization.[3] For many, an excursion to the West was preferred over a trip abroad because there was no fear of seasickness or the obstacle of learning a foreign language.[4] By the 1880s the railroad provided a faster and less expensive mode of travel than stagecoach. Now, leisure travel was affordable not only to the affluent, but also for an increasing number of middle-class Americans, who could afford to take the entire family along.

In increasing numbers, many in the urban middle class sought to get away from their industrial surroundings and to find an escape from the "logical mind and social order." To many Americans, the American West and its native Indians represented true freedom.[5] The railroad took advantage of the rapidly growing leisure market and targeted working-class families. To attract visitors to the Southwest, the AT&SF's new campaign highlighted the healthy climate and agricultural opportunities in Santa Fe and its surrounding area.

Selling Santa Fe to Health Seekers

The AT&SF's first promotional efforts emphasized Santa Fe as a destination for health seekers. Discouraged by the failure of conventional medicine, physicians of the mid-1800s began recommending western health resorts to their patients. By the 1870s, those seeking a healthy environment for relief from tuberculosis and other respiratory ailments found sanctuary in the warm, dry air of southern California.[6] Starting in the 1880s, the Southern Pacific led several promotional campaigns to sell California to the "invalid."[7] The railroad provided special railroad cars and rail-side cottages to isolate tuberculars from healthy patrons.[8] The AT&SF soon followed the Southern Pacific with a campaign of its own.

With regard to New Mexico as a destination for health seekers, Jake W. Spidle, Jr., commented, in his 1987 study *Doctors of Medicine in New Mexico*, that within a very brief period, care for people ailing from respiratory problems became big business in New Mexico, and that this lasted from the 1880s until the start of World War II.[9] The railroad commenced its campaign in 1895 to highlight "lunger" destinations, which included Albuquerque, Socorro, Silver City, Las Vegas, Las Cruces, and especially Santa Fe.[10]

One typical promotional effort featured Santa Fe as a destination for health seekers in a publication called *The New Southwest*, published by the AT&SF in 1890.[11] To persuade tuberculars and asthmatics to visit the "great Southwest country," this brochure touted the town of Santa Fe as "rapidly becoming favorably known as a consumptive sanitarium" because "the combination of pleasant and interesting surroundings, high altitude, and dry, equable, sunny climate [was] proving exceptionally efficacious."[12]

Additionally, to draw people to the city, Santa Fe published its own pamphlet called *Santa Fe as a Health Resort* in 1890.[13] In this publication, the author, Reverend Edward Meany, highlighted Santa Fe as a paradise for health seekers because of its altitude, dryness, and year-round sunny environment, attributes that many believed could cure tuberculosis or consumption.[14] Meany noted that Santa Fe had one of the lowest per-capita death rates from consumption in the United States. Whereas the death rate from tuberculosis in New Mexico was less than 3 percent, fully 25 percent of all deaths in New England and 14 percent of the deaths in Minnesota were from consumption in the previous year.[15] Since the

1880s, both the New Mexico Bureau of Immigration and the AT&SF worked together to advertise the healthy New Mexico climate. In 1883, the Bureau of Immigration had produced a publication for "those in search of health, wealth and homes," including a map of the area and black and white photographs provided by the AT&SF together with a listing of railway service and rail stations.[16]

In 1897, the passenger department for the AT&SF endorsed several health and recreational resorts along the Santa Fe Route.[17] One pamphlet, specifically promoting the health resorts in New Mexico, included information on an array of outdoor activities in Santa Fe such as "horseback riding, burro parties, and walks up and down the hills nearby [which] afford[ed] healthful and delightful recreation."[18] This pamphlet praised the St. Vincent Sanatorium as a comfortable, well-ventilated house with eleven rooms, which offered lunches for "delicate persons" without extra charge. A stay in this well-staffed sanatorium was priced at fifteen dollars per week. A recuperating visitor also had the choice of three hotels. The Claire Hotel could accommodate thirty individuals in rooms equipped with electricity and with access to a complete bathroom down the hall. The cost was twenty to thirty dollars per month, which included room and board. The Exchange Hotel also could sleep thirty individuals and offered the same amenities for thirty-five dollars per month. For those who could afford it, the more upscale Palace Hotel comfortably held one hundred guests, for thirty-five to fifty-five dollars per month, depending on the desired services.

The same publication cited leading authorities who concurred that the altitude, dryness, sunshine, and absence of high winds contribute to "the successful treatment of diseases of the lungs [and] these conditions are to be found at Santa Fe to a marked degree."[19] The pamphlet listed some of Santa Fe's qualities that would heal the sickly:

> The altitude is 6,939 feet; the days are bright, warm and pleasant, and the nights, even in midsummer, sufficiently cool to render blanket covering agreeable. Atmosphere is free from irritating ingredients, containing an abundance of oxygen, electricity and ozone. Drinking water comes from mountains, and is uncontaminated.[20]

How the AT&SF Marketed Santa Fe

Complete with photographs, this pamphlet also highlighted the several hot springs in the area that welcomed guests in winter as well as summer. The "celebrated hot springs of Ojo Caliente" was accessible by a rail trip from Santa Fe to Barranca, followed by a twelve-mile stage trip. A round-trip fare, good for three months, cost a mere $7.50. These springs, which ranged from 90 to 122 degrees Fahrenheit, were considered beneficial to those ailing from rheumatism, paralysis, neuralgia, and consumption.

For passengers on the AT&SF, a leaflet titled "Reasons Why the Santa Fe Is the Most Comfortable Summer Route to California" gave midsummer temperatures of railroad towns along its route. With the highest altitude, Santa Fe offered the most comfortable summer temperatures. With a mean of 66 degrees, and a summer mean daily maximum temperature of 91 degrees, Santa Fe's desirable summertime conditions received considerable attention from the railroad in promoting its namesake town.[21]

Although there are no records available for the number of health seekers who visited the Santa Fe area, the city clearly developed into a popular Southwest resort.[22] As more health seekers began to settle in New Mexico between 1900 and 1920, they provided economic support to build spas and resorts. The extent of this support was such that historian Steven Fox claimed that "Santa Fe [was] made by the railroad and health-seekers..."[23] By 1906 Santa Fe had three sanatoriums to cater to the ailing: St. Vincent, owned by the Sisters of Mercy; the Sunmount, and the Diaz, both privately owned and operated. The AT&SF's *New Mexico Health Resorts* featured these three sanatoriums, which offered comfort and relaxation, and noted that each property employed nurses carefully trained in their profession.[24] The publication also highlighted other points of interest for sightseers, including San Miguel Mission, the Governor's Palace, and local Indian villages.[25] Thus, the AT&SF integrated architectural and cultural themes into its publications in an attempt to further entice health seekers to travel to Santa Fe.

Another popular accommodation for "lungers" recommended by the AT&SF was the Bishop's Lodge, which also catered to people seeking rest and relaxation. A chapel was built on the site in 1853 under the direction of Archbishop Lamy, but in 1905 the renowned Pulitzer family of publishing fame bought the land. They built the lodge and added several other buildings and facilities in subsequent years.[26] In 1921, the Thorpe family purchased the property and turned it into a resort, and in the early 1920s the management of the Bishop's Lodge came under the supervision of the Harvey Company and Jack Vollmar, a man well known to the AT&SF for his administrative skills. Under Vollmar's leadership, the Lodge became a popular "exclusive resort" as advertised by the railroad.[27] In a 1924 article, *The Santa Fe Magazine* promoted the Bishop's Lodge as a "unique and peaceful all-year-round resort for play and rest and comfort."[28] In this article, Vollmar stated his belief "that the Santa Fe region, which in many Santa Fe Railway advertising folders is called the most interesting fifty square miles in America, is the coming resort region of the western country."[29] He pointed out that "the lodge...is in no sense a sanitarium but a place where one can rest or play most comfortably," and that readers of *The Santa Fe Magazine* will find a "hearty welcome" at the Bishop's Lodge at any time of year.[30]

The Santa Fe Railroad focused on various historical and environmental attributes to advertise Santa Fe as a health seeker's destination. For instance, in 1933 *The Santa Fe Magazine* promoted Ojo Caliente in the article "The Oldest Health Resort in America."[31] The author, who suffered from "rheumatic twinges," maintained that the explorer Cabeza de Vaca had named these springs in 1534, though the local Pueblos had previously used them. The author claimed that the Spanish believed they had found the "fountain of perpetual youth," and that over the years the medicinal powers of the spring had continued to soothe and cure thousands of health seekers.[32] Such representation of Spanish and Indian history of the area, regardless of how fanciful, characterized much of the AT&SF's promotional material.

To promote its namesake town, the Santa Fe Railroad produced articles in its employee magazine, as well as pamphlets for distribution, all in a concerted effort to convince people that they needed what the AT&SF had to offer. Those who moved to New Mexico to find relief from lung diseases contributed the first heavy wave of immigration to the state until the 1920s.[33] The AT&SF transported many of these travelers to Santa Fe's higher, warmer, and dryer climate. During the 1920s, it became apparent that it was not the location of the facilities that was important to health seekers, but rather the sanatorium regime, and eastern states began to build their own facilities.[34] Although "climotherapy" began to wane during World War II, with the development of antibiotics, Santa Fe's popularity as a healthy vacation destination persisted. The AT&SF, however, increasingly incorporated new features of the Santa Fe area into its promotions.

Promotion of Real Estate

Of those who traveled to Santa Fe seasonally to recuperate from their ailments, some decided eventually to relocate there permanently. While the railroad provided transportation to those travelers, it also sold them real estate, the proceeds of which helped to pay for the railroad's construction and maintenance. As early as the 1880s, the AT&SF featured a promotional campaign that allowed prospective buyers to see New Mexico for half-price in an effort to entice them to buy land. A Santa Fe flyer from the early 1880s attempted to persuade would-be travelers as follows:

> New Mexico has the oldest improvements; some of the best
> agriculture resources; beyond comparison the finest all-the-year
> climate; the most beautiful mountains and valley scenery;
> some of the richest valleys and finest grazing; the purest air, on
> the continent. She has also SIXTY MILLION ACRES of
> Government Land, aside from all grants and claims, most of
> which has never even been carefully looked at; yet this is THE
> FIRST TIME that Land Explorers' Excursions have ever been
> made to this country.... It is a journey that hundreds make
> every winter for health and pleasure. It can now be done for
> Half-Price.[35]

To entice potential buyers to the area, the railroad called attention to the resources of the land. This is well exemplified in the 1891 brochure *New Mexico: the Land of Prosperity*. Here the railroad boasted of New Mexico as a "most favored spot on earth," and praised "Santa Fe, where the ancient city, nestling among hills, with unequaled climate, the charm of ancient story, and fruit fit for gods, presents a peaceful contrast to the adjacent industries which thrive amid gold, silver, copper, and lead, and precious stones at Cerrillos and San Pedro."[36]

The New Mexico Bureau of Immigration (NMBI) assisted the AT&SF in bringing health-seekers to Santa Fe by producing information in cooperation with the railroad to highlight and sell land to the migrants coming to New Mexico. A bulletin produced by the NMBI in 1898 gave information to home seekers, which featured endorsements from residents, including a cattle rancher, a farmer, and a housewife who boasted of the resources that the area had to offer.[37] By 1909, another pamphlet listed lands in the Santa Fe area owned by the railroad that were for sale, and it gave advice on how to select and obtain a half section (320 acres) for $1.25 an acre, plus filing fees.[38] The bulletin claimed that Santa Fe County had "some of the most fertile spots in the Southwest," and that "the climate is remarkably equable, summer and winter, cool in summer and sunshiny in winter."[39] Some of the foodstuffs raised included apples, sugar beets, vegetables, wheat, and corn. The county claimed fame in its rich grazing lands and mineral wealth. The bulletin noted that Santa Fe was "ideally located as a health resort,"and included a brief historical synopsis of this ancient city.[40]

In 1910 the AT&SF distributed two fact-filled booklets for potential real estate buyers. *Free Lands and Dry Farming in the Southwest* provided detailed instructions on how to secure land through the Homestead and Desert Land acts, and it gave specific information for each county regarding climate, rainfall, and the crops known to prosper there. The publication promoted the fertile land of the area, the ample water supply, and the climate particularly well adapted to growing fruit.[41]

The second booklet, simply titled *New Mexico*, dealt with the irrigation practices used in the area around Santa Fe. The article boasted that alfalfa, oats, wheat, and sweet corn did well in the area, and noted that its celery was simply "the best."[42] Other successful Santa Fe crops that the booklet mentioned included beets, cabbage, beans, spinach, okra, peanuts, rhubarb, squash, melons, and tobacco. Above all, however, "Santa Fe apples [were] famous."[43]

The booklet also provided information on other industries in the Santa Fe area, such as mining. Not far from Santa Fe, the mines of Cerrillos furnished Tiffany's, the famous New York jewelry manufacturer, with its supply of turquoise.[44] Other metals mined in the area included gold, silver, and copper.

New Mexico included a description of the fertile soils around Santa Fe, which supported rich grasslands ideal for ranching. Cattle ranching grew to become big business in the area, and stock could easily be transported by railroad to auctions in stock towns such as Dodge City. Other agricultural industries included dairies and poultry farms. Oddly, the booklet neglected to mention sheepherding, a significant part of the local culture that provided wool for weaving clothing and blankets, which sometimes became souvenirs for tourists, as well as meat for the specialized cuisine of the area.

The AT&SF attempted to lure people to the town of its namesake by providing cut-rate passenger service for those who were considering relocating to the Southwest. The AT&SF rhapsodized about the sunny days, ample rainfall, mild temperatures, fertile soils, and abundant valuable ores, all in an attempt to draw potential farmers, ranchers, and miners to purchase land in the Santa Fe area. The success of this campaign for the city of Santa Fe is difficult to prove, as data on commercial sales are not available. Demographic data show that Santa Fe grew from 4,765 in 1870 to only 7,236 in 1920.[45] The county of Santa Fe also grew relatively slowly, from 9,699 in 1870 to 13,562 in 1890, and to 15,030 by 1920.[46] Thus, both the city proper and the surrounding area grew by just over 50 percent during this fifty-year period. In contrast the population of Tucson, located on the Southern Pacific main line, nearly tripled, from 7,007 in 1870 to 20,292 in 1920.[47] Provo experienced a similar increase during this period, from 3,432 in 1870 to 10,303 in 1920.[48] Perhaps people were curious and wanted to visit and see the native cultures of the area, but they were less inclined to settle among them. An additional reason may be due to the fact that Santa Fe was not on the railroad's main line.

While these data suggest that the Santa Fe Railroad was not successful in its attempt to draw people to Santa Fe, the census data mentioned above do not account for the number of visitors who came only to visit Santa Fe and the surrounding area. Fortunately, numbers do exist for passenger-ticket sales on the transcontinental railroad from Chicago to Los Angeles, and it is likely that many of the travelers en route to California took advantage of their proximity to Santa Fe and the surrounding area with at least a brief visit. At the very least, the continued expenses by the AT&SF to attract passengers indicated that these efforts were successful. Transcontinental passenger-ticket sales increased from $1,785,901 in 1880 to $9,334,661 in 1900, and more than doubled in 1910 to $25,437,181.[49] The Southwest promotions used by the AT&SF may be

linked to producing heavier rail traffic, which in turn generated revenue
for the railroad. And, as will be demonstrated in a later chapter, increas-
es in the numbers of curio shops and hotels provide strong, although
indirect, evidence to suggest that the AT&SF was successful in attracting
people to this region, although demographic data show that most did
not come to dwell there permanently.

Emblems, Icons, and Advertising

From 1900 to his death in 1933, William Haskell Simpson led the innovative advertising campaign for the AT&SF.[50] Created in 1895 by Edward
P. Ripley, president of the railroad, the advertising department, now
under Simpson's direction, hired a group of advertising artists to showcase the Indians of the Southwest, albeit largely from Simpson's stereo-
typed perspective.[51]

In 1908, Simpson's marketing efforts led to the development of a
stylized logo for the Santa Fe Railroad Company as well as individual
insignias for trains on specific routes. [52] As its corporate design, the
company adopted the Zia, the Pueblo sun symbol, which was borrowed
by the state of New Mexico and incorporated into its flag in 1925. The
traditional Pueblo symbol contained a cross with four arms of equal
length, representing the four cardinal directions (north, south, east, and
west), the four seasons (winter, spring, summer, and fall), the four times
of the day (morning, noon, evening, and night), and the four stages of
life (infant, youth, adult, elder), all important elements in Pueblo cultures. Many Euro-Americans saw the Indians as a "cultural artifact" and,
according to Philip Deloria, became envious of the Indian's "true roots"
in America. Furthermore, Euro-Americans perceived the Indians as
"powerful indicator[s] of the timeless and unchanging" civilizations that
found their homes in the Southwest.[53] Capitalizing on this popular
view, the AT&SF used the Zia symbol as a tool to sell the Southwestern
routes.[54] Simpson and his staff had only a superficial understanding of
Indian cultures, and they did not consider the numerous differences
among the many Indian tribes west of the Mississippi.[55] Reflecting this
ignorance, the railroad used the "Chief" emblem, a Plains Indian chief,
to represent both Plains and Southwestern cultures.[56] This design
depicted a "wild," proud Indian brave, adorned with the headdress of a
Plains tribe. In spite of the melding of cultures, the emblem of the Chief

for the Santa Fe Route emerged as one of the most recognizable of all American trademarks.[57]

Before New Mexico acquired statehood in 1912, the AT&SF concentrated on selling the Santa Fe area as a place for settlers and health seekers. The ancient capital of New Mexico was a minor aspect of the railroad's promotional plans as a tourist destination even though the flow of visitors had begun to grow as early as 1910.[58] It would not become evident until years later that this little town off the main line would become a major marketing ploy for the railroad. The lack of promotion in the early years was due mainly to the civic authorities' failure to define or identify the town's attributes, such as its scenic location, distinctive architecture, and diverse cultures.[59] Additionally, easterners may have perceived New Mexico as a wild and untamed land, reflecting its territorial status, and the lack of suitable lodging may have discouraged tourists. Hotel builders, however, saw the need to accommodate more visitors. In 1890, Santa Fe had only three hotels with a total of ninety-five rooms. These were the Alamo, the Exchange, and the Palace. By 1900 the construction of a fourth hotel, the Claire, added another thirty-five rooms. Three of these hotels survived for only a few more years. Nevertheless, by 1911 Santa Fe had a total of five hotels, including the Bishop's Lodge, the Coronado, the Palace, the de Vargas, and the Montezuma, and a total of 150 rooms.[60] The Santa Fe Railroad likely contributed to the demand for more lodging due to its increasingly successful promotion of the city.

Writers and Promoters

The assertive campaign of the railroad to highlight Santa Fe as a tourist destination began after New Mexico gained statehood in 1912.[61] Materials used by the company to market Santa Fe included guidebooks and promotional brochures. These publications reinforced perceptions of the Southwestern culture popularized already in the works of prominent regional writers such as Adolph F. Bandelier, Mary Austin, and Charles Lummis.[62]

A popular novel published in 1890 by archaeologist Adolph F. Bandelier cast the Pueblo Indian as the romantic "noble savage." In *The Delight Makers*, Bandelier "hoped to make the 'truth of the Pueblo Indian' more accessible...to the public in general."[63] Yet Bandelier's book of naturalist fiction portrayed Indians not only as victims, but also as murderers. Nonetheless, *The Delight Makers* likely fed the curiosity of many people who were enticed by the cultures in the Southwest.

Mary Austin's *The Land of Little Rain* (1903) incorporated stories of the denizens of the arid lands in and around Santa Fe, and described the unique type of architecture that combined the building techniques and styles of several cultures.[64] For example, although the AT&SF did not contract with Mary Austin, she eventually settled in Santa Fe in 1923, and may have lured people there with her descriptions of the wide-open skies and poetic accounts of Santa Fe and the upper Rio Grande Valley in her novels *Starry Adventure* and *The Land of Journeys' Ending*. The town of Santa Fe likely gained recognition from her words, and the AT&SF gave people a means of transport to see the town for themselves. Austin claimed that the novel *The Land of Journeys' Ending* was her "monument to...delight in the Southwest."[65] She chose to live in Santa Fe because of "the ancient capital's mountainous setting and nearness to the desert, for its native culture and intellectual sophistication as a gathering place of creative people."[66]

Another important author was Charles Lummis, a Harvard graduate from Ohio who started his career by working for the *Los Angeles Times*. Lummis took a cross-country train ride through the Southwest and sent detailed reports back to the newspaper for publishing.[67] Inspired by the vistas and the people of the area, he also created the travel magazine *Land of Sunshine-Out West* and soon become known as a "one-man tourist agency" because of his enthusiasm for writing about the Southwest.[68]

Lummis, like Austin and Bandelier, romanticized the West, contributing greatly to the creation of the Southwestern mystique. The AT&SF wisely elicited the endorsement of these and other popular authors in its brochures between 1912 and 1940. The strong influence of these writer's works and the growing tourism market led the Santa Fe Railway to commission several of these authors to write brief articles and testimonials for a variety of railroad publications. These pamphlets were designed to acquaint readers with the unfamiliar and fascinating cultures and history of the Southwest.[69]

The promotional work of these prominent writers began to appear in railroad brochures starting in 1912. For example, the AT&SF produced *Old-New Santa Fe and Roundabout*, which included an article by historian and New Mexico politician Ralph E. Twitchell, who touted Santa Fe as "the most picturesque city in the United States[an ancient town] . . . that has given its name to the greatest modern railway system, a name brought to the western continent from Granada, the Magnificent."[70] Twitchell "dearly loved the rich history and traditions of the ancient city."[71] He was a longtime associate of the railroad and mayor of the capital city in 1900, and one of the creators of the Santa Fe Fiesta, the Historical Society of New Mexico, and *Old Santa Fe*, which later became the *New Mexico Historical Review*. Twitchell's views, reminiscent of Austin, Bandelier, and Lummis, are evident in his romantic description of Santa Fe's history:

> Something of that intangible air of mystery that the Moors brought from the Far East to Granada was transplanted to American soil by the conquistadores. There, among scenic surroundings that must have reminded them of their Iberian home, blossomed the City of Holy Faith, the capital of the Sunshine State . . .[72]

For more information on the Santa Fe area, Twitchell suggested that one should "read up" on this "quaint historic city."[73]

Another example of the use of popular authors to promote the Santa Fe area was the 1918 brochure *Santa Fe: The Gateway of the "Greatest Fifty Mile Square in America."* Here, Zane Grey wrote of the beautiful sights and smells of New Mexico. He described the aroma of cedar smoke, the fragrance of the desert sand and dust after a rain, and the "indescribable and exhilarating perfume of the purple sage."[74] Grey noted that thousands of tourists vacationed in Europe every year because they were unaware of the "land of enchantment," and that he pitied those Americans who did not know their own homeland.[75] With these words Grey, who was employed by the railroad, tried to persuade Americans to ride the train to Santa Fe, so that they could become familiar with their own country and take advantage of the recreational and sightseeing opportunities the area had to offer.

Charles Lummis wrote over four hundred books, monographs, and articles on many facets of the Southwest. He founded the Landmarks Club and the Southwest Society, and he was a board member of the

Southwest Museum, which assisted in preserving several of the California missions. The cultures and attraction in Santa Fe and its surroundings also fascinated Lummis. Lawrence Clark Powell considered Lummis "the first and greatest Southwesterner."[76]

In 1923, the AT&SF published *Old Santa Fe and Roundabout*, in which Lummis highlighted the history, cultures, and attractions found in and around the ancient capital. This thirty-eight-page pamphlet included an article titled "Santa Fe: The Capital of Our Romance," in which Lummis praised the marvels of Santa Fe and reminded his readers that "we can build a hundred Chicagos—but all American genius cannot build a Santa Fe . . . [because it is] . . . so swathed with mystery, heroism, reverence, and Romance . . . "[77] His story glorified the violent conquest of Oñate, who brought the first European colonizers to Santa Fe, and told how the conquistador and his men held off "savages" while exploring the frontier. Lummis also extolled the conversion of the natives to Catholicism, pointing out "that eleven missions in and around Santa Fe had already been established before the Pilgrims had landed at Plymouth Rock."[78] His article contained a brief history of Santa Fe, starting with the Pueblo Revolt of 1680, in which the Pueblos slaughtered over four hundred of the twenty-five hundred Spanish colonists in New Mexico. He then related the story of the caravans that moved across the Santa Fe Trail to trade with the colonizers of Mexico's northern frontier between 1821 and 1844, the peaceful American takeover of the capital during the Mexican-American War, and finally the establishment of New Mexico as a territory of the United States in 1851. In this article, his aim was

> to Save the Romance of Santa Fe; to bend the necessities of modern progress so they shall not play vandal to the historic quaintness, picturesqueness and individuality which have been the unspeakable charm and the greatest asset of the ancient capital.[79]

Lummis added a map in the pamphlet's midsection to direct visitors to historically important areas throughout the city as well as other points of interest in the surrounding area, including the pueblos. The AT&SF used Lummis and his knowledge of the area to stimulate the curiosity of potential travelers.

How the AT&SF Marketed Santa Fe

The promotional campaign employed by the Santa Fe Railway System to lure people to Santa Fe may also have assisted in shaping the image of the Southwest by leading prospective visitors to believe that upon their visit to Santa Fe they could step into the past and observe an ancient culture. The *Old-New Santa Fe and Roundabout* touted Santa Fe as a "populous Indian center hoary with age," where tourists could observe Indians on the plaza "ply[ing] their primitive crafts" or performing dances and other ceremonies.[80] One brochure published by the AT&SF in 1927 noted:

> In number and variety, in color and rhythm, the dances of the Southwestern Indians are unsurpassed by the aboriginal ceremonies of any country. Among the Pueblos, living a settled community life through the ages, they [the dances] occur with greater frequency and variety than any other tribe.[81]

The brochure described several dances as "quaint collectives" of Christian and pagan customs and reminded readers that many dances were seasonal and had no specific time to commence, confirming that New Mexico was indeed the "land of mañana."[82] For visitors not familiar with Pueblo customs and beliefs, these dances may have appeared mysterious and archaic. Information presented in the AT&SF's publications may have preconditioned travelers to view the Pueblos in this way and likely helped to confirm widely held Indian stereotypes. By sparking the curiosity of potential travelers and exposing them to Indian traditionalism, the AT&SF provided visitors with an opportunity to glimpse an ancient culture's way of life.

The promotional efforts by the AT&SF also emphasized the Spanish explorers, conquistadors, and missionaries who put their mark on the area and its people. As will be discussed later, Santa Feans would bring back a fiesta, called the De Vargas Pageant, to celebrate the Spanish conquest.

Another tool that the railroad used to market Santa Fe was *The Santa Fe Magazine*, published for the employees of the railroad and other interested readers who subscribed to it. The magazine was similar to *Land of Sunshine* (later renamed *Way Out West*), edited by the popular author Charles Lummis.[83] The latter magazine carried articles on travel and attractions nationally, the writings of popular western writers, and an array of advertisements, many of which were for railroad companies. Appearing to duplicate the format of Lummis's magazine, *The Santa Fe Magazine* began publication in the early 1900s, but advertised the Santa Fe Railway System exclusively.

To inform potential travelers about the various destinations that the railroad company promoted, the company maintained an annual advertising budget. Unfortunately, *The Santa Fe Magazine* did not share with its readers the amount spent on the annual Southwest campaigns or other regional promotions, although it did note that the railroad spent ten million dollars on its nationwide advertising campaign in 1915.[84] By 1922 the railroad company had revised its budget and was able to cut costs by using major publications for advertising; that year the railroad spent over $281,700 on newspaper and magazine ads alone.[85] Owing to the strategies used in marketing the company, the *Santa Fe Magazine* noted, "Results count. . . . [The railroad] has seen for itself—a steadily increasing volume of passenger traffic, a constant addition of new trains and of new cars to the individual trains."[86] In March 1923, *The Santa Fe Magazine* noted that advertising costs had never been a preoccupation of the AT&SF. It spent the bulk of its promotional money on "printer's ink" by running ads in other publications such as *Land of Sunshine*, *Publishers Weekly*, and *National Geographic*.[87]

The railroad exploited the many facets of Santa Fe to attract visitors to the capital city by hiring prominent regional writers to contribute their own experiences and views of northern New Mexico. With the help of these writers the AT&SF was effective at conveying a particular impression about the rustic capital's architecture and culture that distinguished Santa Fe from the desert towns of Tucson, Phoenix, and Los Angeles, the river city of San Antonio, and the West Coast port of San Francisco. As early as the late 1880s, the officers of the AT&SF had recognized the growing interests of travelers who wanted to see the unique landscape of the arid Southwest, and packaged these environmental attributes in the form of publications to inform people who wished to relocate, recuperate, or relax.

As Santa Fe became an increasingly popular destination in the late 1880s and into the early 1900s, passengers continued to journey by railroad to visit the town. However, better services were required to

How the AT&SF Marketed Santa Fe

accommodate these visitors, and Fred Harvey would help make the long train ride more comfortable and enjoyable. A contract between Fred Harvey and the AT&SF in 1889, granting Harvey exclusive rights to manage the railroad's lodging and eating establishments along the tracks, would provide good food and comfort, making the long trip cross-country more enjoyable.[88]

Chapter Three

THE PROMOTION OF SANTA FE BY THE HARVEY COMPANY AND THE AT&SF INTO THE 1930S

Fred Harvey and the AT&SF: The Early Years

Born in London in 1835 to a Scottish-English couple, Fredrick Henry Harvey became famous for his restaurants and hotels and as the most influential partner of the Santa Fe Railway in promoting the city of Santa Fe.[1] At the age of fifteen, Harvey left England bound for New York with ten dollars in his pocket. He quickly found a job at a restaurant paying two dollars a week.[2] Harvey saved his money and bought passage to New Orleans, where he landed another restaurant job. In 1855, with a few dollars saved, he headed to St. Louis, where he opened an eating establishment with a partner. In 1860, Harvey married Barbara Sara Mattas.[3] The couple struggled through hard times, and the outbreak of the Civil War put Harvey and his business partner out of work. Harvey and his wife moved to Leavenworth, Kansas, where he worked in a mail car on the railroad. He became a western freight agent and worked part-time soliciting advertising for the Leavenworth newspaper. In this job, Harvey was subjected to eating at railroad lunch stands, which generally provided "railroad pie," sandwiches, and coffee.[4] There was little incentive to offer better services at these stands. Many of the eateries served poor-quality food, and they often presented an unsanitary environment. Harvey became determined to provide better food and a pleasant atmosphere; he found a partner in Jeff Rice and opened two eateries in the early 1870s, located in Hugo and Wallace, Kansas.[5]

The partnership dissolved shortly afterward, leaving Harvey in need of another partner. He approached Charles F. Morris, superintendent of the AT&SF, who approved of offering good food to passengers at stops along the tracks. In 1876, Harvey used the money he had gained from his dissolved partnership with Rice to purchase an old restaurant at the Topeka Depot, which he soon opened as his first Harvey House.[6] The AT&SF provided Harvey with supplies and the patronage at the depot in Topeka, and under Harvey's ownership and management the eatery became a success. With good food, fresh tablecloths and napkins, the restaurant quickly rose to a step above the standard eating establishments found along the rails, which generally served only chicken potpies and cold sandwiches.

The AT&SF, pleased with his success, decided to support Harvey further and to help him expand his business. The railroad company leased Harvey an old hotel in the town of Florence, near Topeka, and the Harveys provided the linen, silverware, cooking equipment, and walnut furniture. Harvey hired a chef and paid top prices for quality foodstuff. Soon christened the Florence House, Harvey's newest eatery became a popular stopover. The hotel, owned by the railroad, provided lodging and Harvey supplied the food service. During this time, Harvey maintained his position as a freight agent with the Burlington Railroad. He quit in 1882, when he received the concession from the AT&SF to operate all of the hotel and eating establishments on the AT&SF system. Known as "the Harvey Houses," these establishments proved popular not only for travelers on the railroad, but also for locals who enjoyed a delicious meal at a reasonable price.

Even after the death of Fred Harvey in 1901, his eating establishments and hotels continued to prosper. Harvey's son, Ford, took over the hotel and restaurants until his death in 1928, when his younger brother, Byron, became president of the company.[7]

An important facet of Harvey's notoriety came from the popularity of the famous Harvey Girls.[8] These "young women of good character, attractive and intelligent, ages eighteen to thirty," were under a company contract that stipulated, among other things, that they could not marry for one year.[9] In most cases, the Harvey Girls who waited until their contract was over married well, and many married employees of the AT&SF. The Harvey Girls worked for $17.50 a month, plus tips, and the Harvey Company provided the girls with room and board.[10] Many of the girls sent their money back home to help their farming parents.[11] When a train arrived, the crisply attired Harvey Girls worked as long as it took to get the passengers fed. Each girl served eight to ten people for every train that rolled into the depot. For many of the girls, training took place at two of the busiest train stations, located at Topeka's Harvey House and at the depot eatery in Gallup, New Mexico. These women faced an intense thirty-day training program and could not collect a paycheck until they began their duties at an assigned Harvey House.[12] In addition to basic hostess and waitress techniques, the women learned tidbits about the attractions and history of the area of their employment, which they could then pass along to their customers.

As the Harvey Company grew, it became more involved with tourism and marketing its facilities in the Southwest, and promoting the town of Santa Fe was an example of reciprocal assistance between the AT&SF and the Harvey Company. Starting in the 1920s, La Fonda Hotel developed into a vital component of the AT&SF and Fred Harvey team, complete with its own contingent of Harvey Girls. In addition to waiting on tourists and travelers who dined or stayed in the hotel, these young women offered information on the sightseeing excursions provided by Indian Detours, the tour company owned and operated by the AT&SF. In celebration of the 1692 reconquest of New Mexico, an annual Fiesta was held in September at La Fonda. For the celebration, Harvey Girls wore colorful Mexican and Indian-styled skirts and blouses while serving guests in the dining hall or on the open-air patio. They also presented information about the Indian Fair and other events that were included in the Fiesta's itinerary. At other times, these women in their black dresses with white aprons answered visitors' questions regarding things to see and do in Santa Fe, and like the Indian Detours couriers discussed later in this chapter, the girls helped the AT&SF in its efforts to market the city as a visitor destination.[13]

La Fonda of the AT&SF and
Fred Harvey Company

La Fonda, one of the finest Harvey Houses, came to be known as the most famous of the Fred Harvey rail hotels, and ironically, was not located on the main line.[14] Built in 1921 on the historic site of an inn (*la fonda*) that had been established around 1609 to accommodate travelers, La Fonda maintained its landmark location at the end of the Camino Real. For a brief time the hotel carried the name of The United States Hotel, bestowed upon it by General Kearny,[15] but residents of Santa Fe simply called it *La Fonda Americana*. Later renamed The Exchange, the hotel continued to be a well-known landmark and place to socialize.[16] Purchased by Dr. Robert H. Longwell for twenty thousand dollars in 1881, the inn was considered quite a real estate bargain for the time.[17] In 1912 a fire destroyed it, and the remaining structure was leveled in 1919 to make room for the current La Fonda.[18] In 1920, to fund the construction for the new hotel, the Santa Fe Builders Corporation issued $200,000 in stock and divided it into four thousand shares, at $50 each, which were sold to several prominent Santa Fe residents.[19] Commissioned for this important job was Isaac Hamilton Rapp, who designed the new building in Santa Fe Style.[20]

Opening in 1921, this new hotel, owned by local investors, became famous for "the purest Santa Fe type of architecture and [it would soon] be one of the most truly distinctive hotels anywhere between Chicago and San Diego."[21] This unique design, which "combined old Spanish with the native Indian ... [and] came to be known as Santa Fe-style," could also be seen in the Santa Fe Art Museum, constructed three years earlier by architects I. H. Rapp, W. M. Rapp and A. C. Henderson. This unusual architecture was different from the California Mission Style, which was represented by the Alvarado Hotel at Albuquerque, the El Ortiz at Lamy, the Castañeda Hotel at Las Vegas, New Mexico, and several other depots along the AT&SF track.[22] Other famous Harvey Houses that copied Rapp's Southwestern "Santa Fe style" of architecture included the El Navajo at Gallup, New Mexico, and the La Posada at Winslow, Arizona, all located on the main line.[23] The only Harvey House found on a spur was the El Tovar Hotel, at the Grand Canyon. This inn also displayed a "Santa Fe-style" interior, reflecting the Southwestern motif for which Mary Colter later became well known.

Figure 3: Exchange Hotel, ca. 1880. Courtesy of the Museum of New Mexico, neg. no. 39368.

Figure 4: La Fonda, 1927. Photograph by T. Harmon Parkhurst. Courtesy of the Museum of New Mexico, neg. no. 10688.

Figure 5: South Portal of La Fonda. Photograph by T. Harmon Parkhurst. Courtesy of the Museum of New Mexico, neg. no. 54327.

Whereas the exterior of La Fonda gave the appearance of a pueblo, the El Tovar's design gave the impression of a rock and wood lodge.

Unfortunately, La Fonda operated for only two years before delinquent bills and poor management forced it to close its doors.[24] After La Fonda sat dormant for two years, the Santa Fe Railway purchased the hotel in 1925 for $165,000.[25] The Santa Fe and the Harvey Company next commissioned a Santa Fe artist to paint murals of local scenery and culture on the lobby walls. In 1926, the AT&SF hired an interior designer, Mary E. Colter, to redesign the interiors of La Fonda. She engaged varied artistic elements, which included local art, Indian and Hispanic handcrafts, rustic walls and floors, and wooden-beamed ceilings.[26]

Mary Colter was born in Pennsylvania and grew up in Minnesota, where she cultivated an interest in Indian art from a young age.[27] She graduated from the California School of Design in 1890 with a degree in art, design, and architecture.[28] Since 1902 Colter had worked for the Harvey Company to redecorate the Indian Building at the Alvarado Hotel in Albuquerque, and by the 1920s she had designed

H-3551 LA FONDA, THE HARVEY HOTEL AT SANTA FE, NEW MEXICO.   AFTER PAINTING BY FRED GEARY

Figure 6: La Fonda Postcard. Courtesy of the Museum of New Mexico, neg. no. 177667.

the interiors of several Harvey Houses. Writer Erna Fergusson commented that Colter "studied Southwestern architecture and all its variants from church to pueblo, from Moorish castle to Navajo Hogan, and she incorporated all their features into Harvey's hotels.... She...brought the work of the Southwestern artists and rare examples of Mexico and Indian pottery and of hand-carved saints in the bedrooms."[29] Colter incorporated these eclectic decorations and construction materials in Harvey Houses throughout the Southwest. One visitor who was smitten with La Fonda reported his experience to *The Santa Fe Magazine*:

> Last summer some good angel directed my wandering footsteps to La Fonda in Santa Fe. One expects the best as a matter of course at Harvey hotels; but I was not prepared for La Fonda. Evidently the rising generations of Harvey Hotels are given a college education before appearing in public. Architecturally La Fonda is the apotheosis of adobe. Otherwise it is everything a modern hotel should be, plus unanticipated refinements of comforts.[30]

As an interior decorator, Colter borrowed a motif that combined Spanish and Indian styles. Unlike the many depots that had been built to represent the "California Mission style" of architecture, La Fonda featured ceilings supported by exposed wooden *vigas* (beams) and adobe walls lined with colorful Mexican tilework that represented the area's Hispanic heritage.[31] Colter also "promoted and paid homage to Indian Art" by displaying intricate baskets, colorful rugs, beautiful pottery, and intriguing sand paintings that decorated the hallways and lobby area.[32] In 1929, the hotel was enlarged to accommodate the influx of tourists who participated in the Indian Detours tour service.[33] For visitors, La Fonda provided the Courier Lounge, containing a comprehensive library on sites to visit and things to do in Santa Fe.[34] And in the Indian Lecture Lounge, Harvey Girls, couriers, or informed lecturers spoke in the evenings on Spanish and Indian history, or on local points of interest.[35] Tourists at La Fonda also could observe Indian women weaving rugs, or purchase handcrafted Indian arts at the hotel's curio and gift shop.[36]

Because of the beautiful collection of art within its walls, La Fonda grew to be one of Santa Fe's favorite attractions. The AT&SF purchased or traded works of art, for rail fare or lodging, with individual artisans, or purchased the art through collectors employed by the railroad, such as Herman Schweizer, or Indian traders like Lorenzo Hubbell. The AT&SF and the Harvey Company amassed one of the best collections of western art in the United States and showcased various pieces of the collection in La Fonda and other Harvey Houses and depots along the Santa Fe routes. Several of the paintings in the collection were reproduced to decorate brochures and pamphlets promoting Santa Fe and the Southwest.

Fostering the Art Colony

The AT&SF and the Harvey Company contributed greatly to the promotion of Santa Fe by displaying artistic works that depicted scenes from in and around Santa Fe.[37] In the process, "the railway helped to establish and nurture the artists' colonies in both Santa Fe and Taos."[38] From the time the railroad spur connected Santa Fe to the main line, a number of artists began to make their living by painting the area's picturesque landscape.[39] The railroad provided passage and board to several painters it commissioned to sketch Santa Fe-area scenes for the company's advertising campaigns and popular publications.[40]

The Promotion of Santa Fe

In 1892, the AT&SF employed its first two artists: Thomas Moran, an immigrant from England, and Fernand Lungren, from Maryland.[41] With no formal art training, Moran began his career as an illustrator for magazines, including *Harper's* and *Scribner's*. He later traveled with survey teams through Yellowstone Park, painting the geysers, hot springs, and cliffs, and he became known not only as a painter but also as an expedition artist because he recorded the landscapes and scenery in the park through his sketches.[42] Lungren studied at the Pennsylvania Academy of Fine Arts and the Academy Julian in Paris and, like Moran, worked as an illustrator for *Harper's*. Both Lungren and Moran painted various Southwestern landscapes and subjects along the rail, including the Grand Canyon and the Pueblos around Santa Fe. William Simpson, the advertising manager for the AT&SF, used their paintings to advertise the spectacular landscape of the arid Southwest. These works appeared on company brochures and a variety of other promotional material.[43] Annual visits from the two eastern artists to the Southwest produced numerous works of art, among which several were used to promote rail travel in the Southwest. Some of the other railroad artists lived in New Mexico only during the warmer months, and the railroad provided their transportation to Santa Fe and their meals at La Fonda in exchange for their artistic works. Other painters, however, relocated permanently to Santa Fe.[44]

One of the railroad's artists, Eanger Irving Couse, gained recognition for his work through publications produced by the AT&SF, which commissioned twenty-two of his works.[45] His paintings first appeared on the 1914 calendar produced by the AT&SF, and they were featured continuously on calendars from 1916 to 1938.[46] Another artist, Gerald Cassidy, initially moved to Albuquerque in 1890 as a health seeker suffering from tuberculosis, but he eventually relocated to Santa Fe in 1912.[47] In 1915, Cassidy received international recognition for his works when he won the grand prize, in the fine arts competition, for his murals of the rock at Ácoma, the Enchanted Mesa, and the cliff dwellings at Pajarito that were displayed at the Indian arts exhibit at the Panama-California Exposition in San Diego. The Santa Fe Railway and the Museum of New Mexico, in a combined effort, sponsored this exhibit. For years, reproductions from many of Cassidy's works decorated railroad postcards and travel posters. One of his paintings, "La Fonda—The Inn at the End of

Figure 7: Map Painted by Gerald Cassidy in La Fonda. Photograph by Edward Kemp (AT&SF Railroad). Courtesy Museum of New Mexico, neg. no. 53752.

the Trail," promoted the hotel in the 1929 *Indian-detour* brochure. Additionally, Cassidy painted many of the murals in La Fonda, including the regional map, which is still located in the foyer close to the entrance of the hotel, and was also featured in the 1928 edition of *Harveycar Motor Cruises: Off the Beaten Path in the Great Southwest.*[48]

Another Santa Fe artist who assisted in La Fonda's decoration in 1928, Olive Rush, painted flowers and vines around doorways, murals on walls, and decorated glass windows. Other artists who lived in Taos and contracted with the railroad in the 1910s and 1920s to paint Santa Fe-area scenes included Louis Akin, Joseph Henry Sharp, and Bert Greer Phillips. Several of the works from each of these artists also appeared on railroad calendars that were distributed throughout the country. These pieces used for reproduction in promotional materials became part of the Harvey Collection.[49]

Santa Fe emerged as an art colony several years after Taos, which was founded in the late 1890s, and remained smaller than the artistic center to the north. Consisting of only five artists in 1915, the Santa Fe art colony grew slowly with the addition of Cassidy, Rush, and others in the 1920s.[50] Often employed by the railroad, these painters concentrated on village scenes, landscapes, and Indian and Hispanic subjects.

The Santa Fe colony became an important component of the AT&SF's tourism campaign. As the number of railroad travelers began to increase in the 1920s, so did the number of paintings that they purchased.[51] The Indian Detours tour company assisted in stimulating the art colony by taking tourists to studios and arranging rendezvous with the artists at La Fonda.[52] Travel magazines and newspapers increasingly featured articles and pictures, which further popularized the Santa Fe area.[53] With its beautiful scenery, distinctive cultural heritage, and fascinating history, Santa Fe became a retreat for both artists and writers, as well as a major tourist attraction.[54] Tourism grew into an important industry for Santa Fe in the late 1920s, and Santa Fe artists prospered because of their increased exposure to railroad travelers.[55]

The Depression affected travel and tourism and in turn reduced exposure of the demand for artistic works, making it difficult for artists to maintain their livelihoods in the profession. Additionally, several prominent artists employed by the AT&SF passed away in the 1930s, leaving Santa Fe without several of its founding art-colony members. Though the number of artists slowly dwindled away, their paintings still survive.

By 1940 the AT&SF had collected over five hundred pieces of artwork that it had commissioned since 1892. Today, many of these paintings remain in collections open to the public, including the Heard Museum in Phoenix, the Atchison, Topeka, and Santa Fe Railway Museum in Schaumburg, Illinois, and the Kansas State Historical Society in Topeka. These works served as important elements in promoting the Santa Fe area to cross-country travelers who found themselves admiring the Southwestern scenes that hung on the walls of depots and railway stations across the nation.

Indian Detours and Fred Harvey Company

Rail service, followed by the advent of auto travel in the early 1910s, helped to keep the "picturesque" town of Santa Fe, with its deep-rooted heritage, as a destination for tourists. This interest was interrupted during World War I as railroads became the main method for transporting military men and equipment, and passenger services received a low priority. Consequently, "luxury train service" was cancelled in 1919, but it resumed in 1920.[56] Additionally, automobile production declined as vital resources were allocated to the military.[57] After the war auto travel to Santa Fe once again became popular. In anticipation of the expected surge of visitors, the city of Santa Fe added 205 rooms with the completion of the Bishop's Lodge in 1920.[58]

Before 1925, passengers on the Chicago to Los Angeles route were offered a free side trip to Santa Fe, including a night's stay at the De Vargas Hotel. In 1925, the cost for a roundtrip fare from Chicago to California was $143.78 per person. Chicago to Santa Fe was only $78.85.[59] That year the AT&SF and the Harvey Company led a major new promotional effort to sell Santa Fe as a tourist destination. This new campaign included a tour of Santa Fe that gave travelers a respite from the long train trip across the country, while offering the railroad a means to generate extra revenue.[60]

The first bus to be used to escort tourists between Lamy and Santa Fe arrived in Santa Fe in late 1925, via rail from Chicago. In the same year, preparations were made to stem the decline of railroad passenger service caused by intense competition from auto travel. Ford Harvey and his Harvey House operation joined forces with the AT&SF to organize a tourist service called Indian Detours.[61] Established to sell the Southwest to travelers, Indian Detours was a quasi-independent company with an independent staff and offices. The founder of this innovative company was Major R. Hunter Clarkson, whose father-in-law was vice-president of the AT&SF.

Clarkson, a native of Scotland, had volunteered for duty in the Royal Flying Corps in 1914. After service in France, Egypt, Russia, and Italy, he retired to a farm in Scotland in 1919. During his retirement, he met an employee of the Harvey system who suggested that Clarkson relocate to the United States.[62] Accepting this challenge, he found work in the Harvey Company as a transportation manager at the Grand Canyon in the early 1920s. While working in Arizona, Clarkson met and married the daughter of Arthur G. Wells, the railroad's vice-president, and became enraptured by the landscapes and cultures of the Southwest. He particularly was attracted to New Mexico, with its "Indian ruins in abundance, the oldest city in the

The Promotion of Santa Fe

United States, and a wandering river whose name was synonymous with romance."[63] In 1924 Clarkson conceived the idea of setting up a three-day motor tour that included the area between Las Vegas, New Mexico and Albuquerque, and he began organizing an excursion program in cooperation with the AT&SF. The sightseeing company soon monopolized the tour-car market in Santa Fe as the Fred Harvey Company had at the Grand Canyon.[64] Clarkson's innovative tour service provided travelers a closer look at the environment than could be seen through a train window, and offered access to places unreachable by railroad.[65]

With the purchase of La Fonda by the AT&SF in 1925, additional rooms became available for the optimistic expectations of the new tour company. To commence the 1926 tour season, Clarkson announced the Indian Detours sightseeing service nine months early, on the twenty-ninth of August, 1925, in the *Albuquerque Morning Journal*, noting that "the announcement is considered one of the most important [announcements] ever made in modern railroading in that for the first time in history a transportation system will be operating a rail and bus system in parallel lines over a great part of the territory."[66] The following day the *Albuquerque Journal* ran a column captioned, "Fifty Thousand Tourists Will Traverse State." The article announced a large-scale advertising campaign for Indian Detours by the AT&SF and Fred Harvey Company, and that La Fonda in Santa Fe would be the tour headquarters.[67] To advertise the new tour company, the AT&SF printed the first *Indian-detour* brochure in November 1925.[68]

Clarkson busied himself through the fall and winter of 1925 with the final preparations for the first trip of the tour season, which was to take place on May 15, 1926.[69] Newly hired and trained local drivers, or "dudes" as the tour company tagged them, helped to work out scenic routes. These drivers were hired because of their knowledge of northern New Mexico, and those who spoke Spanish received higher consideration. Additional duties of the dudes included minor auto repairs along the route and digging out vehicles that became stuck in mud holes or sandy arroyos.[70] The dudes also kept strict records on each car, including oil changes, tune-ups, and flat tires.[71] To advertise these tours of the Santa Fe area, the new tour company produced an additional array of promotional items including postcards, calendars,

Figure 8:
*Sights to See
along the Santa
Fe* (Chicago:
Rand McNally
& Co., n.d.).
Courtesy of the
Kansas State
Historical Society,
MSS RR Box No.
883, Folder 11.

maps, and brochures.[72] These materials depicted old missions and pueblos, blanket-clad Indians among adobe buildings, and the distinct architectural style found in the area. The brochures also included information on the locations and histories of pueblos.

To showcase the Southwest, this service included tours to many of the Pueblos located in the areas of Santa Fe and the Grand Canyon, but Santa Fe was the hub of the activities.[73] A promotional brochure dated 1926 declared, "It is the purpose of the Indian Detours to take you through the very heart of all this [Indian country], to make you feel the lure of the Southwest that lies beyond the pinched horizons of your train window."[74] Beginning in May of 1926, Indian Detours planned to offer a three-day tour, including meals and rooms at La Fonda Hotel, for the price of forty-five dollars.[75] Clients could choose one of the three itineraries, and after their tour, they were escorted back to the mainline at Lamy to continue their transcontinental journey.

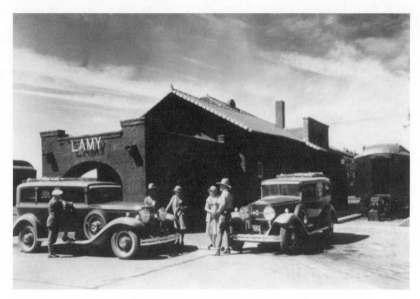

Figure 9: Harvey Cars at Depot, Lamy, NM, ca. 1930. Photograph by Edward Kemp, Courtesy of the Museum of New Mexico, neg. no. 53651.

Figure 10: Harvey Car at Santa Clara, n.d. Courtesy of the Museum of New Mexico, neg. no. 46940.

The tour service was a smashing success. In an article in the *Albuquerque Morning Journal* travel writer Ottillia M. Halbach wrote that "every bend of the road, every turn of the mountainous sky line, every change in the shifting sunlight effects were eagerly anticipated by the group. There were many bends in the road, many striking light and shadow effects, many inundations in the skyline—many delightful surprises—for the tourists in their three days of life in the 'Land of Yesterday.'"[76] The same newspaper also reported that an Australian traveler mentioned the comfortable rooms, the good service, and the "lovely country"; a woman tourist from New Orleans noted that La Fonda "is a beautiful hotel—it's so rough and primitive looking with all the necessary comforts"; and a Miss Seelye, a traveler from Kansas, said that she did not "believe there [was] a thing that could be done to improve the trip."[77]

The Indian Detour tour service was patterned after an Albuquerque company, Koshare Tours, owned by Erna Fergusson, a well-known author of New Mexican history and sister to New Mexico novelist Harvey Fergusson. Founded in 1921, Koshare Tours was purchased by the AT&SF in 1926, and because of Miss. Fergusson's expertise she remained on board to assist in running the tours and to train female guides.[78] Fergusson preferred female guides because she believed that they were more talkative and comfortable with people than were men.[79] Required to have a grasp of Spanish and understand geography and geology of the region, the guides were also required to know the archaeological and ethnological history of Santa Fe and its surrounding pueblos and points of interest.[80] If the couriers were fluent in another language, such as Maria Baca was in Spanish, or Margaret Wennips in German, they received additional pay.[81] Because of her attention to detail and her knowledge of the area, Fergusson became known as an expert tour guide.[82] One tourist wrote a tribute to her on a sheet of La Fonda stationary, in the form of a poem about his tour experience with Fergusson as his guide.[83] Fergusson resigned in 1927, but Winifred Schuler, one of Indian Detours's knowledgeable guides, took over with the same thorough preparation.[84] The *Harveycar Motor Cruises* pamphlet made note of the knowledge and services of the guides:

> Greeting guests on their arrival by train, it is thereafter the
> Couriers' privilege to fill the pleasant dual role of hostesses as

Figure 11: Indian Detour Couriers—Margaret Wevaign, Hazel Miller, Farona Konopek, Mary Tucker, 1928–29. Courtesy of the New Mexico State Records Center and Archives, Konopek file.

well as guides. Their information is not intruded; it is simply a store of remarkably interesting facts. . . . Friendships with representative Indians in many pueblos assure their guests intimate glimpses of Indian life not otherwise obtainable.[85]

Schuler selected uniforms for the guides, or "couriers," which included pleated walking skirts and velveteen blouses fashioned after traditional Navajo dress.[86] She also asked the couriers to wear concho belts, squash-blossom necklaces, and other Indian jewelry, thereby enticing visitors to purchase Indian arts and crafts while touring the Pueblos.[87] The couriers also assisted in luring people to the Santa Fe area with their unique sightseeing service. Indeed in an effort to persuade passengers to take one of the tours, several of the enthusiastic couriers rode the trains between Chicago and Los Angeles to distribute brochures on Indian Detours.[88]

The couriers became very popular and known both for their charming personalities and their knowledge of the area. In 1928, Clarkson

Figure 12: Drivers for Harvey Car Motor Cruises, ca. 1929. Courtesy of Museum of New Mexico, neg. no. 106937.

received a letter from Benjamin F. Shamaugh, who wrote of his experience on one of the tours and offered high praise for Mrs. Wendling, a Santa Fe courier; Shamaugh noted she "seems to understand people with whom she is traveling and adjusts herself to them very tactfully and very charmingly.... [and she was] ever mindful of the interests and comforts of her guest on the trip."[89] That same year a woman from New York complimented Miss Hubbell, another courier, whose "interest in her work did much to enhance our pleasure."[90] Another letter mentioned that Rita Brady, Mary Heller, and Margaret Wennips "made us feel at home at once. Their quiet, interesting way of imparting information and describing points of interest certainly added to the pleasure of the trip."[91]

In addition to being successful, the couriers also enjoyed their jobs. One guide, Emily Hahn, was the first woman to receive a Bachelor of Science degree in Mining Engineering from the University of Wisconsin, in 1926. After earning her diploma, Hahn worked briefly for a St. Louis lead and zinc mining company where, because of her sex, she was only allowed to do office work. With a desire to see the world, she soon

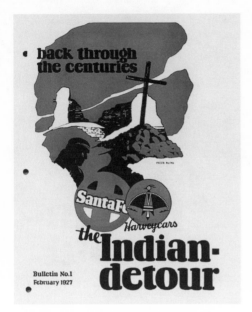

Figure 13: *Bulletin No. 1*
(February 1927). Courtesy
of the Burlington Northern
Santa Fe Railway, "back
through the centuries."

moved to Santa Fe to work as a tour guide.[92] Hahn wrote of her experiences while working and living in Santa Fe in the summer of 1927:

> Santa Fe was not merely my state of mind. It was really an
> interesting place—possibly the only town of its kind anywhere.
> You couldn't dismiss it as a resort for pleasure seekers, because
> it is also the state capital, as well as a refuge favored by doctors
> for tuberculosis cases. Santa Fe was a mecca for American
> Indian experts, being a living museum of Mexican and Indian
> culture. Most of all, it was an artists' colony. These differences
> didn't leap at once to the eye—I doubt if my Detour dude saw
> them—but Santa Fe was a rich, rare city to live in.[93]

Hahn later became a world traveler and a prolific writer, documenting her experiences from around the globe in fifty-two books as well as several articles in *The New Yorker*.

These tour guides and their hospitality left visitors with fond memories of their vacation in Santa Fe, and many of these travelers likely shared their enthusiasm about their trip with friends and relatives.

Figure 14: *Bulletin No. 2*
(August 1927). Courtesy of the
Burlington Northern Santa Fe
Railway, "the Indian-detours."

Whether by word of mouth or by the railroad-advertising program, it was evident that the tourist industry in Santa Fe had increased in the late 1920s from the previous decade.[94]

The subsequent influx of tourists in 1927 resulted in a 169 percent increase in patronage at La Fonda from the previous year.[95] To accommodate those visitors, La Fonda was enlarged over the next two years. Although no statistics are available to document the success of the Indian Detours campaign, the increase in hotels and curio shops between 1920 and 1940 may be a testament to the marketing efforts of the AT&SF and the Harvey Company.[96]

The advertisements that the AT&SF used for Indian Detours reached people nationwide. A 1928 advertisement in *National Geographic Magazine* said that "cruises lasting from days to weeks, start from La Fonda Hotel in Santa Fe . . . [and that] schedules may often be arranged to include colorful and unusual Indian ceremonies, in the heart of the famous 'Indian-detour country.'"[97] An ad in the same magazine a year later called *Indian-detours* "a motor-link unique in transcontinental rail travel."[98] The nationwide campaign likely helped to lure tourists to the capital city, so that they could experience the cultural charm and mystique

The Promotion of Santa Fe

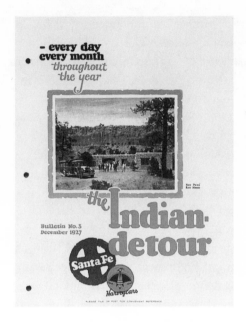

Figure 15: *Bulletin No. 3* (December 1927). Courtesy of the Burlington Northern Santa Fe Railway, "every day, every month, throughout the year."

of Santa Fe and the surrounding area. The Indian Detours itinerary provided the opportunity for visitors to see more of the area than most travelers had seen before.[99] Passengers could leave the train at Las Vegas, New Mexico, and take a three-day excursion to Santa Fe and the surrounding area, staying both nights at La Fonda before visiting Albuquerque on the third day, prior to resuming their journey to California. For eastbound travelers, the reverse route was available.[100] Another option was to take the daily train from Lamy directly to Santa Fe. Indian Detours picked visitors up at La Fonda and escorted them by "Harveycar" on tours within Santa Fe, to surrounding Pueblos such as Pecos, Tesuque, and San Juan, and to the Puyé cliff dwellings.[101] Taos Pueblo was added to the list of tours in 1928.[102] Tours provided visitors with opportunities to observe Indian ceremonies and dances. By 1929 the success of the tour service allowed the company, in consideration of the passenger's comfort, to purchase new Cadillacs and special buses. These new vehicles gradually replaced the old Packard motor pool and proved to be both rugged and dependable.[103]

The stock market crash of 1929, which occurred after the tour season, did not have an impact on the company until the following summer when people began to show less inclination to travel. After the death of

Ford Harvey in 1928, moreover, his brother Byron decided to sell Indian Detours to compensate for operating losses. The transfer of Indian Detours from the mother company, Santa Fe Transportation, a subsidiary of the AT&SF, to the new owner, Major R. Hunter Clarkson, also manager of the Santa Fe Transportation Company, took place on March 15, 1931.[104] Renamed Hunter Clarkson, Inc., or simply referred to as "Detours," the company continued its relationship with the AT&SF and the Fred Harvey Company, even retaining its headquarters at La Fonda.[105]

Despite the onset of the Depression, over forty-seven thousand tourists took the Santa Fe tour in 1930, and Clarkson said "he would not be surprised to see the number doubled" in 1931.[106] Toward the end of the Depression, Americans began to travel again, and tourism returned as a prosperous industry for Santa Fe. Yet by the mid-1930s Clarkson's tour service had lost its momentum. Equipment started to age, many people could no longer afford the luxury of a chauffeured, guided tour, and Detours provided more luxury than most visitors needed or could afford. By 1937 Clarkson's company suffered from loss of patrons because of the popularity and increase of "drive-it-yourself vacationers" who preferred to make their own itineraries.[107] Additionally, starting in the early 1930s, the AT&SF advertising department ceased printing the *Indiandetours* brochure annually and discontinued several of its other brochures, such as *Roads to Yesterday* and *Harveycar Motor Cruises*.[108]

Nevertheless, by the early 1930s the Santa Fe Railroad had already put Santa Fe on the map as a tourist destination, and it can be argued that it was the marketing efforts of the railroad that set the stage for subsequent growth for tourism in Santa Fe. Although people still traveled, now they crossed great distances in the comfort of their own vehicle. With no direct route by rail, Santa Fe was now accessible by interstate highway, making it a thoroughfare for auto travelers. Thus, in spite of the decline in railroad business, tourism in Santa Fe continued to increase, which was reflected in the increase in lodging facilities. Whereas in 1929 the capital city had five hotels, by 1940 eleven hotels were available to visitors.[109] Another indicator of the resulting growth of tourism in Santa Fe was the increase in the number of curio shops, from seven in 1929 to seventeen in 1940.[110] In 1940 the Work Projects Administration report for New Mexico noted that Santa Fe's major industry in the 1930s had been the tourist and vacation trade.[111] Most likely, some of this growth reflected the number of visitors influenced

What do *you* know about the Forgotten Peoples of **Pu-yé** and **Ci-cu-yé** of Pueblo Bonito and Penasco Blanco~of Aztec and Mesa Verde?

WHILE WESTERN EUROPE was yet a wilderness, prehistoric American peoples wove fine cotton cloth, built great irrigation systems, reared many-storied cities. Mystifying ruins from that time-dimmed past dot the magnificent mesa and canyon country of New Mexico and Arizona. Here in America, among primitive Mexican villages and Indians of many tribes, is an undreamed-of American history, romance and antiquity.

Harveycar Motor Cruises now open up this little known territory. Packard Eight Cruisers, with Harvey-trained driver mechanicians. A courier-hostess accompanies each party, limited to four persons in one car.

Cruises, lasting from days to weeks, start from *La Fonda Hotel* in Old Santa Fé. Cars, however, will meet parties at any point on the Santa Fe transcontinental lines between Trinidad, Colorado, and Grand Canyon, Arizona.

Schedules often may be arranged to include colorful and unusual Indian ceremonies, in the heart of the famous **Indian-detour** country.

Harveycar cruises are operated throughout the year. Rates $25.00 per day per person, for parties of three or more, include every expense.

Mail Coupon—

Santa Fe

Harveycar Motor Cruises *Harveycars*
Santa Fé, New Mexico
Please send me information regarding Harveycar Motor cruises.

Harveycar Motor Cruises
Under Santa Fe-Harvey Co. Management
1015-A   Santa Fe', New Mexico

Figure 16: Ad in *National Geographic* (June 1928). Courtesy of the Burlington Northern Santa Fe Railway.

by the variety of promotional campaigns employed by the AT&SF and the Fred Harvey Company in the late 1920s and early 1930s, such as Indian Detours and the array of publications produced to highlight Santa Fe.

As the country began to climb out of the Depression, dreams were shattered by the announcement of war on December 7, 1941. From that moment on the AT&SF and the Harvey Company assisted in the war effort. The federal government restricted nonessential transportation and suspended all sightseeing tours. Additionally, with the death of Roger W. Birdseye in December 1942, the AT&SF and Harvey Company lost the talented and insightful advertising manager who had developed the general publicity for the AT&SF and Indian Detours campaigns. Indian Detours would always be remembered, however, as a unique and first-class sightseeing tour company to those who got a glimpse of the scenery, history, and cultures in and around Santa Fe.

Cultivating Culture and Crafts

An important aspect of the Indian Detours promotion of the late 1920s and 1930s was highlighting Native American culture of the Santa Fe region.[112] The Harvey Company and the AT&SF used two methods to demonstrate Southwestern Indian life. Both methods capitalized on the Navajo people from western New Mexico and local Pueblo people who gathered in Santa Fe to display their crafts. One method showcased the "living" Indian found weaving in the hotel lobby or dancing at a nearby Pueblo, while the other displayed native works in the railroad depot and in hotel lobbies such as La Fonda's. The "Indian Room" adjacent to the lobby area in La Fonda housed a particularly superb assortment of old Spanish, Mexican, and Indian handcrafts, all a part of the Fred Harvey collection, many of which were available for purchase.[113] These items included famous Chimayó weavings, Indian-made blankets, silver jewelry, pottery, and *santos*—Spanish religious figures carved from wood.[114] Yet the Indian arts and crafts for display and for sale far outnumbered Spanish and Mexican pieces.[115] William Wroth, a writer and collector of Hispanic crafts, commented, "Hispanic crafts never 'caught on' nationally the way that Indian crafts did."[116] The showcasing of Indian culture on the promotional materials and on tour itineraries created by the AT&SF may have contributed to the popularity of Indian crafts over the work of other ethnic groups, and was exemplified by the sales of these items, which grew rapidly starting in the late 1920s.[117]

Figure 17: Candelario's Curio Shop, 1905. Photograph by T. Harmon Parkhurst. Courtesy of the Museum of New Mexico, neg. no. 10730.

Figure 18: La Fonda's Curio Shop, ca. 1927–28. Photograph by T. Harmon Parkhurst. Courtesy of the Museum of New Mexico, neg. no. 54319.

By giving Indian crafts a "unique art status" and making them popular souvenirs for tourists, the railway and the Harvey Company effectively used their influences to create and manipulate the Indian arts market.[118] Herman Schweizer, supervisor of the Curio Department at La Fonda and the person in charge of the Harvey Collection and Indian Department, began commissioning jewelry for eastern wear in 1899 and hired silversmiths to produce inexpensive silver trinkets.[119]

Before the promotion of Indian jewelry by the AT&SF and Harvey Company few Indians could afford to buy the tools and materials required to mass-produce silver jewelry and other Native items. As more travelers ventured into New Mexico wanting mementos of their travels, the AT&SF and Harvey Company recruited Pueblo artisans to make Navajo-style silver jewelry.[120]

Under the guidance of Schweizer, the AT&SF and the Harvey Company promoted their own kind of commercial industry by establishing Indians as skilled artisans, who then modified their jewelry, pottery and baskets, by scaling down the size of the items, for the tastes of eastern parlors.[121] By 1931 the Indian Room at La Fonda began to compete in the sale of inexpensive souvenirs with Woolworth's, the dime store located only a couple of blocks away and across from the Plaza. La Fonda was forthright, however, in telling its customers if the pieces were not native, and it continued to carry an array of fine crafts for collector enthusiasts.[122]

Frank Clough, who headed the Railway News Service for the Harvey Company, voiced anxiety in a letter to Schweizer over the volume of cheap imitation jewelry that Woolworth sold to visitors in Santa Fe.[123] Schweizer was also concerned about Indians who purchased jewelry at Woolworth for fifteen cents and sold the same item to tourists for $1.50.[124] Curio shops also sold cheap mass-produced native crafts during the Depression that were made by non-Indians.[125] In September 1931, the man in charge of the Indian Department for the AT&SF, J. F. Huckel, informed Schweizer that the Federal Trade Commission had prosecuted a firm in the East for false advertising in Albuquerque because it was selling Pendleton robes as Indian robes.[126] Such false-advertising charges could also apply to imitation Indian jewelry being passed on as original handcrafted Indian jewelry.

Another person concerned with commercialization of Indian crafts was Detour courier Emily Hahn. In her memoirs, she recalled a conversation with roommate and fellow courier Ann Cooper in 1927, regarding her concerns with the curios that were being sold:

> Tourists do ruin Santa Fe. Think of the herds we [the tour company] bring in and take around, think of the junk they [the tourists] buy.... Those terrible little kachina dolls. You can't find genuine ones anymore. And look at the Navajo silverwork. It's going to hell, because the Indians don't bother when they can sell any old thing.[127]

In regard to protecting naive tourists against the purchase of unauthentic crafts, Schweizer mentioned that some of the Indian traders in the area were supporting the Frazier Bill, which called for the protection of authentic Indian crafts by marking them with an official stamp.[128] In September 1932, John F. Huckel, founder of the Fred Harvey Indian Department in Albuquerque, wrote to Schweizer with his concerns about souvenir jewelry:

> when you were here... I showed you quantities of old silver of pawn which you say is quite reasonable, but this is not what the great mass of people want. They consider it quite high. Until the Navahos [sic] learn to make silver by improved methods a[n] old ring at $5.00 was considered cheap. People now want the similar ring for $1.50, and an old bracelet weighing one ounce in what we call pawn that has been worn will sell for about $4.00. The people want a bracelet for $1.50.[129]

Railroad officials made conscious efforts to offer travelers both authentic and inexpensive souvenirs representative of the Southwestern cultures. The success of the Santa Fe Railway and Indian Detours in generating business for Indian arts and crafts likely is reflected in the increase of curio shops.[130] In Santa Fe, for example, the number of curio shops increased from four to eighteen between 1920 and 1940, suggesting that the market for trinkets and souvenirs was increasing.[131]

No campaign in the nation surpassed the AT&SF and the Harvey Company's advertising of Indian arts and crafts or native culture. This use of culture as a promotional tool attracted the attention of several writers.[132] Among them, Leah Dilworth wrote, "these two modern corporate entities, which were paragons of efficiency and marketing, wrapped themselves in an Indian blanket, so to speak, and used Indians to 'naturalize their activities.'"[133] In *Dream Tracks: The Railroad and the American Indian*, T. C. McLuhan wrote that "with their [Indian Detours] ads extolling a 'newly found' culture of a 'gentle, peaceful and picturesque people' who lived a 'nature-loving' way of life, the AT&SF admen created the impression that they were the saviors of a lost civilization."[134] By romanticizing the Pueblos in art reproduced for advertising, and by molding native handcrafts to suit eastern parlors, Santa Fe and the Harvey Company reconstructed and publicized the Pueblo lifestyle in a version of Indian life that reflected what the railroad and Harvey Company believed middle-class Americans wanted to see.[135] And for many travelers, Santa Fe was the place to observe the romanticized version of Indian life. To this day, Santa Fe continues to display its distinct cultures and permits local Indians to peddle their crafts to visitors under the portals surrounding the Plaza.

Although the promotional efforts of the AT&SF focused primarily on Indian culture, one Southwestern tribe was notably absent from the advertising campaign. Some contemporary historians suggest that the nomadic Apaches apparently did not appeal to tourists who were more interested in a glimpse of the "romantic" and "conquered" Pueblos, rather than the "warlike" Apaches.[136] If visitors perceived Apache culture as "hostile" in nature, the AT&SF may have consciously determined to glorify the "gentle" and "docile" Pueblos and Navajos in the railroad's marketing effort to sell the Southwest.[137]

Although some tourists no doubt visited Santa Fe to observe Spanish and Mexican cultures, the representation of both of these peoples was virtually absent from railroad promotional materials after 1910.[138] In the rare cases when the railroad acknowledged the Spanish and Mexican presence in its travel literature, it glamorized the daily life of these cultures.[139] The AT&SF projected the stereotypes of Mexicans and Spaniards featured in dime novels such as those published by *Beadle's Dime Library* in the late 1800s.[140] In *Old Santa Fe and Roundabout*, the railroad enticed tourists by describing the "common sights" on the city streets of Santa Fe—"pinyon-laden burros," dark-eyed women and children, and men who smoked their "cigarros" while "doffing" their sombreros to passersby.[141] This brochure also provided a short history of the Spanish and Indian influence on Santa Fe and the distinctive blending of Spanish, Mexican, and Pueblo cultures in Santa Fe. This mixing resulted in a particular character that permeated local cuisine, customs, and art.[142] All of these cultural features were used by the AT&SF to promote its namesake town; a town not on its own rail line, and these components contribute to the town's popularity to this day.

The marketing strategies of the railroad in the late 1920s and early 1930s were probably most influential in showcasing Santa Fe as a visitor destination. By targeting the Southwestern cultures as an attraction, the AT&SF generated a means of recovering revenues lost because of the popularity of auto travel. Additionally, by acting as the intermediary through the Indian Department, the AT&SF was able to profit in the production and resale of Indian arts and crafts. By the mid-1930s, marketing efforts by the Santa Fe Railroad would begin to decline, but tourism in the ancient capital would continue to increase.

The Fame of Chimayó

The role of textiles in the tourist trade began to grow once the railroad reached Santa Fe. This began with Indian rugs and blankets and later included Mexican and Hispanic designs as well. In the 1920s, several of the curio shops in Santa Fe sold Spanish and Mexican curiosities as well as Indian handcrafted items.[143] These shops included The Emporium, the Old Mexico Shop, Spanish Arts, and the Spanish and Indian Trading Company.[144] One shop listed in the 1940 *Santa Fe Directory* sold Chimayó rugs and blankets, and these weavings were available at a couple of Harvey Shops in New Mexico.

Known for their distinctive hand-weavings, these were made by the Hispanic villagers from Chimayó, not far from Santa Fe. In the early 1900s, however, the artists of Chimayó were threatened by the commercialization of the textile industry. The AT&SF played an important role in resurrecting this artistry, although it could be argued that selfish investors motivated the interest in local crafts. By the 1920s curio dealers in Santa Fe began to put the weaver's skills to use for the tourist trade and Chimayó weavings became an important commodity.[145]

The Chimayó rugs and blankets reflect over three hundred years of the village traditions that began in 1540, when Coronado's expedition brought several thousand sheep into the area. New Mexico proved to be a hospitable place and the sheep thrived to become an important part of the Spanish colony's economy, providing both food and wool. Located close to a Tewa Pueblo, the villagers of Chimayó exchanged goods with their Pueblo neighbors.[146]

Nicolas Gabriel Ortega was born in Chimayó in 1729, and he began a family tradition of weaving that would last for over five generations.[147] In 1805 Spanish authorities sent Mexican master weavers, under contract for six years, to Santa Fe, to improve the weaving skills of colonists.[148] After they completed their contract the weavers relocated to Chimayó and worked with the Ortegas to establish a weaving center.[149] Chimayó blankets became important trading items and thousands were exported to Mexico.[150] Domestic use as well as commercial needs led to the development of a substantial industry, employing sheepherders, spinners, and weavers. The arrival of commercially spun cotton and wool in 1880 made spinning obsolete, but the finished piece was less durable with cotton yarn. Most threatening for the Chimayó weavers was the arrival of commercial mill-woven blankets brought by rail, making their village trade almost obsolete. However, the local weavers still continued to weave colorful hand-dyed blankets for their families, and the people of Chimayó held to their traditional beliefs and customs, which have existed for centuries.

In 1919, the Museum of New Mexico, with other sponsors including the AT&SF, organized the annual Santa Fe Fiesta; a three-day event intended to highlight the Spanish and Mexican cultures of the region. The Spanish Market, which featured Chimayó weavings along with other crafts produced by local Hispanics, became part of the Fiesta program in 1928.[151]

The Santa Fe Railroad developed important ties with local groups such as Chimayó artists and the art colonies. These relationships helped the communities to sell their products, while these products were used by the railroad to attract visitors, thereby translating to tourist dollars. Thus, the relationship between the railroad and the artists is a classic example of a commercial mutualism, with both partners benefiting through the interaction. Chimayó weavings remain a popular tourist commodity and they continue to be sold in shops in the Santa Fe area as well as the Old Town Plaza in Albuquerque.[152]

Chapter Four

PROMOTING SANTA FE THE AT&SF WAY—THEN AND NOW

The Santa Fe Fiesta

In the 1930s, the AT&SF continued advertising Indian Detours and La Fonda, but the railroad also started to branch out to promote other attractions and events.[1] While continuing to publicize historical sites, the AT&SF began sponsoring cultural events. To attract people to the old capital, the AT&SF helped to revive and to promote an important celebration called the "Santa Fe Fiesta." Established in 1712, the Santa Fe Fiesta was held only sporadically thereafter, gradually disappearing from the Santa Fe social calendar. After a lapse of 150 years, Edgar L. Hewett, director of the Museum of New Mexico, revived the Fiesta in 1919.[2] In 1920, the Santa Fe Fiesta came under the auspices of the School of American Research, with Hewett as the Fiesta's director.

Born on a farm in Illinois, Hewett became a teacher in Missouri's Tarkio College, soon rising to the position of college president.[3] He later moved to Santa Fe and began promoting the cultures of New Mexico as early as 1903. With funding from the Archaeological Institute of America, Hewett established the School of American Archaeology in Santa Fe. By promoting the school with an objective of encouraging new enrollment, he drew attention to the town of Santa Fe and the fascinating cultures found in the area. Some historians believe Hewett to be the individual most responsible for putting Santa Fe in the national spotlight, and the Santa Fe Fiesta was one way to showcase the town.[4]

The Santa Fe Railway, however, was the first company to market the town as a tourist destination. Long before the revival of the Fiesta, Hewett had maintained a close working relationship with W. H. Simpson, advertising manager for the AT&SF. Hewett provided black and white prints of Pueblo archaeological sites for reproduction in the AT&SF brochures; in return, Simpson gave train travelers copies of the summer school bulletin for the School of American Archaeology in Santa Fe.[5] The AT&SF also assisted Hewett in promoting the Fiesta by offering discount rates to tourists who wished to experience the three-day celebration, which was restructured to give each of the three major ethnic groups of New Mexico a day of celebration. The railroad provided free advertising by including articles about the event in its own publications.

The August 1920 issue of *The Santa Fe Magazine* featured an article promoting the Fiesta and urging visitors to attend. The article promised "those among our readers who spend their vacation in and about Santa Fe and viewing this fiesta will never regret it. It is the ultimate in something different."[6] The following month the same magazine reported that "last year's three day event was marvelous in its interest and beauty."[7] The Fiesta program in 1919 offered a glimpse into "three great bygone ages of the Southwest—the Indian, the Conquest, and the Martyr epochs."

On the first day, Saturday, a parade of "braves" from surrounding Pueblos performed dances and presented various religious dramas on the Plaza in front of the Palace of the Governors. These presentations included the "Race of the Rain Clouds" and "Painting of the Flutes."[8] Each Pueblo performed dances, including Tesuque Pueblo's "wonderfully significant and mystic Basket Dance" designed to greet autumn and the return of water to the earth. The Taos Pueblo presented its "famous Sunset ceremony, which [was] the most charming episode in the San Geronimo Fiesta," held annually in September.[9] The evening of the first day ended with Spanish dances by performers attired in costumes from Castile and Aragon.[10]

On Sunday, the Fiesta focused on the Spanish conquistadors, who reached Santa Fe almost eighty years before the Pilgrims set foot on

Promoting Santa Fe the AT&SF Way—Then and Now

American soil. The day also celebrated the reconquest of 1692, when Don Diego de Vargas took Santa Fe back from the Pueblos for recolonization. A demonstration called the De Vargas Procession, led by a lineal descendant of de Vargas "in gorgeous costume," celebrated the reconquest of Santa Fe.[11]

Monday, the third and last day, bestowed honor to the Franciscan martyrs, and included a memorial parade for the padres who were killed before and during the Pueblo Revolt of 1680. The event that evening concluded at a grand ball with guests costumed in Spanish and Mexican attire. The author of one article boasted that the entertainment would be "unique and extraordinary even for America." *The Santa Fe Magazine* article enticed rail travelers to the area by rhapsodizing:

> Santa Fe in itself, most attractive and distinctive among cities
> of the Southwest, offers much in its immediate surroundings
> in the way of mountain and mesa landscape, forests and
> canons, cliff dwellings and mission churches, pueblos and
> plazas. . . . [The Fiesta] is the opportune time to visit this
> unique city and enjoy a spectacle that is gorgeous and
> fascinating beyond words.

Writing about the modern Fiesta's second year, Charles Parks referred to the 1920 celebration as "firmly established" and "one of the most beautiful historical pageants in the United States."[12] He added:

> It is an axiom of the West that its mysterious charm cannot be
> evaded. By many it is compared to a disease—a slow fever,
> with the sensation of pleasure substituted for that of pain.
> The casual traveler—the mere passerby—suffers a slight
> attack, which even the confinement of a Pullman cannot pre-
> vent. . . . The real tourist—that hardy personage who sets out
> to explore and to investigate the cañons, the desert and the
> mountains, or to wander among the primitive races and the
> prehistoric dwellings of a forgotten age, often suffers an acute
> attack. Chronic symptoms appear when the tourist turns to
> the systematic collection of Indian, Spanish or prehistoric
> relics and curios.[13]

The author continued the article with a descriptive history of Santa Fe, claiming that Spanish rule from 1700 to 1822 was "marked with constant Indian warfare."[14] Yet he claimed that the Fiesta now marked a joining together of these cultures. For many of the Pueblos that participated in the reestablishment of the Fiesta in 1919, this was the first time in their history that Pueblo dances had been performed away from the sacred kiva.[15] And they would return to dance from that year onward. The article also included several photographs of Pueblo dances and festival activities. By showcasing the local Pueblo culture, the Fiesta also provided an attraction to travelers and in turn helped stimulate passenger ticket sales for the AT&SF.

For the 1922 Fiesta, the AT&SF contributed a float designed as a replica of a locomotive. In the March 1923 issue, *The Santa Fe Magazine* published a picture of the parade entry, along with photos of the officials from the Santa Fe Railroad who accompanied the float in the parade.[16] Although the town was not on the AT&SF main line, the railroad company took great pride in showcasing its namesake town.

The Santa Fe Fiesta program for September 1–3, 1924, announced reduced rates on rail travel to Santa Fe.[17] The back cover of the program contained a full-page ad called "Off the Beaten Path," and included information on how to obtain the railroad brochure *Old Santa Fe and Roundabout*, which accentuated the other popular attractions of Santa Fe.[18] The program also contained advertisements for La Fonda, promoting it as a "home for tourists" during the Fiesta.

The Fiesta coordinators featured a new twist for opening night in 1926. Santa Fe artist Will Shuster created "Zozobra," or Old Man Gloom, a large figure made of stick and papier-mâché.[19] The stick figure had been introduced in 1924, and then burned in Schuster's backyard during the Fiesta.[20] The following year Zozobra grew to eighteen feet tall, and by 1926 it had become part of the Fiesta program. The effigy was set on fire to cast aside worry and gloom. From that time on, "Zozobra" and the opening bonfire remained an integral part of the Fiesta.[21] The Fiesta program for 1926 included a reprinted article by Charles Lummis, courtesy of the Santa Fe Railroad. Titled "The Capital of our Romance," the essay featured a descriptive history of Santa Fe. The author compared Santa Fe to Tucson, fully 171 years younger, and he observed that no other town north of Mexico had a history to match that of Santa Fe.[22] The same publication included various advertisements from hotels and curios shops, and displayed a full-page ad on the back cover for the AT&SF's Indian Detours, including excursions especially for "fiesta visitors."[23]

In 1926, *The Santa Fe Magazine* article "Re-discovery of Old Santa Fe" informed readers that "everyone in Santa Fe wears Spanish costume during Fiesta week, and it is a joyous, fun-loving people who welcome the strangers within their gates with open arms, and with charming courtesy make them feel at home.... The lure of the Indian country is great. Every visitor to Santa Fe vows that he will return someday."[24] Photographs of the attractions in and around Santa Fe accompanied the message that "there is always something stirring 'round about old Santa Fe.'"[25]

In 1925, Thomas Wood Steven, who worked for the AT&SF advertising department, moved to New Mexico's capital and became an eager advocate of the pageant. In 1927, Hewett put Steven in charge of a dramatization called the "Pageant of Old Santa Fe."[26] Additionally, the Fiesta, which had previously been held in mid-September, was now changed to the first week of September to attract more tourists over the Labor Day holiday.[27] *The Santa Fe Magazine*, published by the railroad, promoted the Fiesta in a variety of ways: it romanticized the history of the ancient city, glamorized its people, and promoted the excitement of the Fiesta as a means to persuade people to visit the town during the three-day event.[28]

The largest financial donor to the Fiesta in 1930 was La Fonda.[29] In return, the Fiesta program included advertisements for La Fonda, and AT&SF ads for Indian Detours again covered the entire back page of the program. In 1935 the AT&SF produced its first brochure designed exclusively to publicize the Santa Fe Fiesta. It included a brief history of the town and paid homage to its distinct architecture by drawing attention to La Fonda, which was the center of "the gaiety and color of the Fiesta."[30] The brochure also included black and white photographs of many of the events during the three-day ceremony.

By 1939, the Fiesta continued as a well-organized event.[31] In October of that same year, *The Santa Fe Magazine* ran a five-page article recounting the festivities. Even with the grim news from Europe that the war had started—though not for the United States—Santa Fe was "filled to

Figure 19: Zozobra, 1942. Courtesy of the Museum of New Mexico, neg. no. 47328.

overflowing as usual, with hotels and private homes crowded," and the "[i]nternationally famed hostelry, La Fonda, was the center of the gay pageantry and social activities."[32] The Fiesta commenced with the burning of the forty-foot figure of Zozobra, still constructed under the guidance of local artist Will Shuster. Attended by leaders of the "social and official life of the city, and hundreds of visitors, all garbed in historic and striking costumes," the *Gran Baile* at La Fonda was the place to socialize on the last evening of the Fiesta.[33]

The Santa Fe Railway assisted in promoting the Santa Fe Fiesta nationally. By featuring articles in the railroad magazine and advertising Indian Detours in the Fiesta programs, the AT&SF continued to focus attention on New Mexico's capital city while seeking to generate passenger sales and to entice travelers from across the country who wanted to participate in the September festivities. For those who wished to travel by automobile, Indian Detours still offered a closer look at the local cultures and the surrounding landscape.

The Santa Fe Fiesta continues to attract people from all over the world. The Santa Fe Convention and Visitors Bureau publicizes it as "the

Figure 20:
San Miguel
Misson, 1950.
Photograph by
Tyler Dingee.
Courtesy of the
Museum of
New Mexico,
neg. no. 91839.

oldest continually observed event in the United States."[34] Now a week-long celebration, the Fiesta remains much the same as it was seventy years ago, commencing with the burning of Zozobra and ending with the Procession to the Cross-of-the-Martyrs. And of course the *Gran Baile* continues, although now this takes place on the Plaza. Arts and crafts are available for purchase and visitors can still wander through the twisted roads around the Plaza to observe the sites of Santa Fe, including the "Santa Fe Style" architecture exemplified in the surrounding buildings.

Santa Fe Style

Some of the popular attractions in Santa Fe today include its old buildings, churches, and missions, which give the town its historical ambiance. As early as 1912, the AT&SF depicted many of these structures in its brochures either in the form of illustrations or in brief historical descriptions of the buildings.[35] By using Santa Fe's architecture

Figure 21: Portal at Palace of the Governors, n.d. Courtesy of the Museum of New Mexico, neg. no. 6851.

as an attraction, the railroad had yet another hook to lure travelers to the ancient capital. To understand the significance of the "look of Santa Fe" and why the AT&SF frequently featured these old structures, one must look at the builders and the material used in the construction of the first buildings in the capital city.[36] Before Spanish contact, the Pueblo people in the area built sturdy villages containing flat roof houses of poles and mud.[37] With the arrival of the Spanish, few structural changes took place in large part due to lack of alternate building materials.[38]

The Palace of the Governors became one of the popular old buildings publicized by the Santa Fe Railway. The history of the structure commenced in the early 1600s, when the Spanish viceroy directed Governor Pedro de Peralta to fortify Santa Fe. In response, Peralta designated one block of streets for government buildings and erected a royal palace. When completed, the royal palace housed "1,000 people, 5,000 head of sheep, 400 head of horses, and 300 head of cattle without crowding."[39] Its three-foot-thick adobe walls provided protection from intruders and stabilized other structures that were attached to the walls.

Promoting Santa Fe the AT&SF Way—Then and Now

Peralta's headquarters, dubbed the Palace of the Governors, is the oldest government building in the United States, and it dominated one side of the plaza.[40] Built in what is now called "Spanish Colonial," the Palace's specific type of adobe architectural style was employed by the Spanish in the construction of churches and public buildings across New Mexico for over two centuries.[41] This style, evident in the Mission of San Miguel in Santa Fe, built in 1610, and in the church of Chimayó, erected in 1816, borrowed the flat roof and mud (adobe) construction from the Pueblos, although the Iberian influence is reflected in the ground level door, corner (kiva) fireplace, and the vigas (roof timbers) that added structural strength for larger rooms.[42] Typical residential buildings consisted of a single room with an attached shelter. For the more affluent, several rooms encircled a central patio, or *placita*, which generally contained a well.[43] One room, the *sala*, was used to entertain guests and became the sleeping quarters at night; another room served as the kitchen; and one room may have served as a storage area.[44] Rooms could be added on to the house as the family grew.

Zebulon Pike visited Santa Fe in 1807. He described the town as a "fleet of flat-bottomed boats," and referred to it as "a hazard collection of flat-roofed houses constructed out of adobe clay."[45] At this time, encircling the Plaza of the long, narrow town, lay several one-story buildings, including government offices, an inn, a few stores, and private residential quarters.[46]

Because of its isolation, Santa Fe received few material goods from Mexico. After the advent of Mexican independence in 1821, the citizens of Santa Fe began to trade with the United States for building materials and other goods. Door hinges, saws, and other metal tools made construction much less labor intensive. After the Mexican-American War, the so-called "Early Territorial" style gained popularity. Remodeled to this new style, several buildings in Santa Fe added windows with glass and white-painted wooden trim. Examples of this design can still be seen on some of the buildings facing the Plaza in Santa Fe. The railroad also brought new building materials to Santa Fe including fired bricks, lumber, cast-iron columns, and glass windows, along with an array of milling tools.[47]

As new ethnic groups moved to Santa Fe, they began to share their building techniques. One example is the St. Francis Cathedral, built in

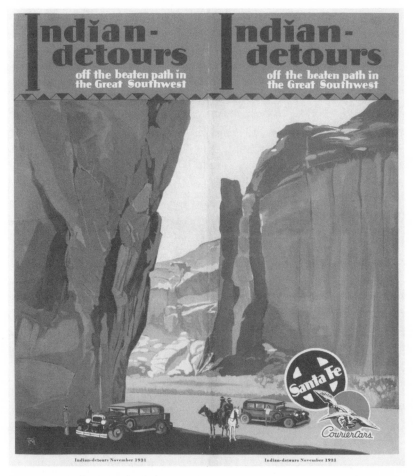

Figure 22: *Indian-detours*, November 1931. Courtesy of the Center for Southwest Research, University of New Mexico, MMS (BC) Box 1 Folder 14.

1869 under the direction of the Frenchman, Archbishop Jean Baptiste Lamy. The church represented the fine Byzantine-styled cathedral of Marseilles in his homeland, and differed starkly from the adobe buildings found in the Santa Fe area.[48] The Loretto Chapel, featured in several railroad brochures, was built between 1874 and 1877, consisted mostly of quarried stone, and was modeled after the Saint Chapel in France; this gothic-styled chapel also was quite different from the common adobe missions built throughout the area.[49]

Promoting Santa Fe the AT&SF Way—Then and Now

With the advent of railroad transportation, Santa Fe was flooded with a variety of architectural styles and materials to select from. The Plaza of Santa Fe, however, remained much the same, even though Gothic and Queen Anne styles skirted the Plaza area. By the early 1900s the Spanish Pueblo, Pueblo Revival, and Territorial styles, later all called the Santa Fe Style, gained popularity, and many of the original buildings were restored to their initial design.[50] The town implemented a design-control ordinance in the 1930s that endorsed architectural uniformity for new structures built in Santa Fe.[51] The "Pueblo" or "Territorial" Revival style of building became specific to Santa Fe, and many brochures of the AT&SF included illustrations of these structures.[52] The railroad brochures showcased several buildings as attractions for visitors to see during their stay in the capital city.

One of these brochures, *To California Over the Santa Fe Trail*, featured "The Old House, where Coronado [was] said to have lodged in 1540, and the Church of San Miguel, which was sacked in 1680. Both represented, according to the railroad pamphlet, "a petrifaction of medieval human life done in adobe."[53] This booklet also contained illustrations of ruins and buildings that included Pueblo and Spanish architecture. Another brochure, *Old Santa Fe and Roundabout*, described San Miguel Mission as "the oldest church edifice...built in 1636 and restored in 1710."[54] Other buildings mentioned included the Palace of the Governors and the *garita* at Fort Marcy.[55] The first *Indian-detour* brochure, produced in 1925, featured several pictures of magnificent adobe buildings, including the Museum of New Mexico and La Fonda.[56] These pictures illustrated the specialized style distinctive of Santa Fe and appeared in most of the promotional pieces.

In 1927, the railroad brochure *Roads to Yesterday* featured an article describing an excursion taken by a couple who spent six months in Santa Fe. The article claimed:

> They spent their days wandering about the little city unlike any other in the world. They conscientiously saw the Palace of the Governors,...the gorgeous new art museum built in replica of the historic Franciscan Missions of New Mexico, the oldest house and the oldest mission in the United States all of which were as interesting as the railroad circulars proclaimed them.[57]

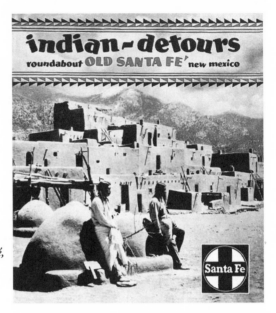

Figure 23: *Indian-detours Roundabout Old Santa Fé, New Mexico.* Courtesy of the Burlington Northern Santa Fe Railway.

This article helped to support the successful marketing efforts used by the AT&SF to persuade visitors to travel to Santa Fe by extolling the incomparable architectural style of the city.

The Santa Fe Magazine, published for the employees of the railroad and other interested subscribers, also discussed the appearance of Santa Fe in many of its articles over the years.[58] In 1932, an article described Santa Fe, "with its narrow streets wandering in and out among warm adobe walls of the homes, set in grounds with clumps of old gnarled cottonwoods."[59] The author explained how Santa Fe "had retained its individuality by slow growth and the pride taken to continue the early style of architecture known as Spanish-Pueblo."[60] The writer paid homage to Santa Fe's own La Fonda:

> This beautiful and unusual building has been erected about a
> sunny, stone-flagged patio of great charm. It has a glorified
> picturesqueness of the ancient pueblos. The interior is allur-
> ing and restful. Throughout in the furnishings are scattered
> priceless pieces from Spain and Old Mexico. Other pieces
> have been created in Spanish-Pueblo style and are decorated

individually to fill the rooms. Large plate-glass mirrors, framed in unique frames of tin, the work of painstaking Mexican artists, are placed all about. Hand-wrought Spanish lanterns hang in the lounges, portals and halls.[61]

Pictures of the historic buildings in Santa Fe covered the jackets of the Santa Fe Railroad brochures. The AT&SF captured this unique architectural style and put it on display throughout the railroad's publications, illustrating the uniqueness of the town among the other popular attractions of the capital city.

Taste of the Southwest

Only in recent years has the taste of the Southwest become an attraction characteristic of Santa Fe. Although a difficult hypothesis to prove, it is possible that this phenomenon developed as a consequence of the Santa Fe Railroad. With the numerous train cars full of travelers that the AT&SF brought to New Mexico, the reputation of the fiery foods of New Mexico is likely to have been spread by word of mouth. Few hotels or restaurants along the track served the authentic New Mexican foods, such as green chile stew, red chili sauce (*not* Tex-Mex), *posole*, *menudo*, and *calabacitas*.[62] These foods are found only in the "land of enchantment," where Santa Fe has maintained its cultural dominion through centuries. Presently, the New Mexico legislature has gone as far as to adopt into law an official state question, "Red or Green?" asked in cafés, restaurants, and homes wherever chile is served.[63]

Spanish colonists first brought chiles to New Mexico in 1598. The original "NuMex" chile is a long green chile that turns red when dried, and is the basis for most of the popular New Mexico cuisine.[64] The sauces consist mostly of chile (red or green), water, garlic, salt, and sometimes flour for thickening.

Visitors to Santa Fe in the early 1900s most likely dined at their hotels since the overnight fee included both meals and board. By 1921, Santa Feans began to promote Spanish or local cuisines in their city directory. For instance, Mrs. Emilia Garcia advertised her Spanish meals, and The Royal Café, owned by Lupe Herrera, offered authentic fare, although she also prepared short-order meals.[65]

Several cookbooks of authentic New Mexican dishes became available by the 1930s. These cookbooks may have been on hand for purchase at the Harvey Newsstand in La Fonda for those visitors with adventurous palates who wished to replicate the spicy foods in their own home. The *Mexican Cookbook* by Erna Fergusson included New Mexican recipes, while under Mexican rule.[66] This book was published in 1934 and very well could have been on hand for visitors when Ms. Fergusson escorted her patrons around the Southwest, when she owned Koshare Tours and later directed Indian-detours for the Atchison, Topeka, and Santa Fe Railroad. *New Mexico Dishes* by Margarita C. de Baca included Spanish foods that were typical of New Mexican fare.[67] A third book, by Cleofas M. Jaramillo, *The Genuine New Mexico Tasty Recipes*, published in 1939 and reprinted in 1942, included foods that were common fare in the 1930s, and many of which remain popular today.[68] The author of this book, born in 1878, wrote the book in hopes of preserving this facet of the Hispanic culture. Fabiola Cabeza de Baca Gilbert wrote *Historic Cookery* and *The Good Life: New Mexico Traditions and Food*, which included recipes that also were distinctly New Mexican in origin.[69] Sadly, few contemporary cafés or restaurants in Santa Fe offer traditional foods such as *pancha, chicos,* or *atol.*[70]

Perusing menus from La Fonda in the 1920s reveals that the fare was prepared more for eastern palates than for the local tastes.[71] They offered such standard meals as grilled fish steak, chicken potpie, braised beef, or omelettes.[72] To accompany the entrée, visitors could select two side dishes from whipped potatoes, hashed browned potatoes, romaine salad, creamed spinach, and new peas. To sample the local cuisine visitors only needed to walk along the Plaza to find a Mexican café, where the locals frequently dined. By 1930, La Fonda offered "*Comida Corrida Mexicana* (a complete Mexican dinner)," either in the *La Placeta* outdoor dining room or inside in the *Cantina*, although brochures do not describe what the meal included.[73] Nevertheless, in 1951, one could order eggs with green chile at La Fonda, and in 1954, the Special Mexican Plate included a taco, tamale, an enchilada, salsa, and a fried egg.[74] A Mexican food menu was also available upon request.[75] By 1956, Byron Harvey Jr. prepared a reference file to his travel and ticket agents, which listed all of his properties and their amenities along the rails. La Fonda advertised a "Complete Mexican Dinner" and featured dinner dancing to La Fonda's own Mexican Orchestra.[76] The Alvarado in Albuquerque made no reference to special or regional cuisine.

To promote some of the fare along the tracks, *The Santa Fe Magazine* published various New Mexican recipes in its column titled "Harvey Girls' Recipes." This was later reprinted as a small cookbook. One recipe featured *Albondigas*, which was somewhat of a green pepper soup with meatballs. Another recipe consisted of *Enchiladas* served with the chile sauce where tomatoes made up one half of the ingredients, and olives garnished the entrée.[77] These recipes are strongly influenced by Europeans, and certainly are not traditional New Mexican foods.

Today Santa Fe is known around the world for the traditional regional foods found there. Within walking distance of the Plaza, Santa Fe offers over seventy-seven restaurants and cafés, 42 percent of which either specialize in or offer New Mexican or Southwestern cuisine.[78] Many New Mexicans still enjoy the same foods that their ancestors prepared centuries ago, and some claim that a percentage of visitors become chile addicts after their stay in Santa Fe.[79] Whether the Atchison, Topeka, and Santa Fe Railroad System contributed to promoting the tasty Southwestern cuisine is difficult to ascertain. Several Harvey Restaurants prepared and served the unique New Mexico cuisine and by doing so they helped to spread the word. This distinctive food is as much a part of the attraction to Santa Fe today as are the cultures that have prepared it over the centuries.

Chapter Five

THE TOWN DOWN THE TRACKS:
SANTA FE'S RIVAL—ALBUQUERQUE

Albuquerque

When the Atchison, Topeka, and Santa Fe first made its way through the northern half of New Mexico, surveyors had determined to bypass Santa Fe because of its location on a high plateau at the foot of the Sangre de Cristo Mountains. The railroad decided the best route for its track would be down the Galisteo Basin to the Rio Grande Valley, leaving Santa Fe on a spur eighteen miles to the north and putting Albuquerque on the main line.

In many respects, Albuquerque resembled Santa Fe before the coming of the railroad. Before the intrusion from Europeans, the Rio Grande Valley was home to several Pueblos. Natives supported themselves largely through farming and by trading with local Pueblo residents and nomads who traveled along the Rio Grande down into Mexico. In 1706, fully 165 years after Coronado first walked through the valley and spent the winter of 1541, Spaniards first colonized the vicinity of current-day Albuquerque with 252 men, women, and children. The villa of *Alburqurque* (the first *r* was dropped a century later) was founded by Governor Francisco Fernández Cuervo y Valdés, who named the town after the viceroy of New Spain, Duke of

Figure 24: Cathedral and Plaza, Albuquerque, New Mexico, ca. 1890. Courtesy of the Colorado Historical Society, call no. CHS J1358.

Alburqurque, who had appointed Cuervo to his post.[1] The new villa was established almost one hundred years after the colonization of Santa Fe. Situated sixty miles south of Santa Fe, Albuquerque lay in a wide valley along the banks of the Rio Grande, where it was possible to ford the river.

Like Santa Fe, Albuquerque was a stopover for people traveling the Santa Fe Trail. Unlike Santa Fe, however, it was neither a main point of entry nor the end of the trail. Santa Fe retained its dominance as the trade and political seat in the territory. Still, much trade from the east continued out of Santa Fe into Albuquerque by way of the Guadalupe Trail, later to be known as the Santa Fe Trail. The main trading items consisted of finished wool textiles and piñon nuts.[2] Also known as a farming and ranching community, Albuquerque produced a variety of delicious fruits and vegetables. Sheep were the preferred livestock raised by ranchers. Because Albuquerque sits at roughly five thousand feet elevation, some twelve hundred feet below Santa Fe, it generally is five to ten degrees warmer in the summer and ten to thirty degrees warmer in the winter, contributing to a somewhat longer growing season.

The Town Down the Tracks

The plaza of Albuquerque sat less than one mile from the river; family land plots, however, were adjacent to the river and used for agricultural purposes. Like Santa Fe, Old Town Albuquerque was laid out around a plaza with *calles* (roads) radiating outward like a spider's web. Construction of San Felipe Neri began in 1793, and this historic church still dominates the north side of Albuquerque's Old Town plaza and remains one of Old Town's chief tourist attractions.

One of Albuquerque's founding families was that of Vicente Ferrer Armijo, who had migrated from Zacatecas, Mexico. His grandson Manuel, youngest of eight children, participated in the Santa Fe trade and later became involved in politics; he served three terms as governor of Nuevo Mexico. Armijo resided in the territorial capital of Santa Fe. His first term (1827–1829) ended prematurely when he resigned to avoid investigations for malfeasance, retiring to his hacienda near Albuquerque until 1837, when he returned to the post of governor in Santa Fe.[3] While Armijo was serving his third term, the Mexican-American War broke out. Armijo surrendered to General Stephen Watts Kearny of the United States Army, and fled to Mexico. Congress subsequently established New Mexico as a United States territory, with Santa Fe as its capital, and Albuquerque continued as a stopover on the Santa Fe Trail.

After New Mexico's entry into the Union in 1846, the population of Albuquerque began to change dramatically, with the influx of American citizens from the eastern states.[4] Native woolen mills were modernized with metal parts transported over the Santa Fe Trail. In the 1850s, Simon Rosenstein and Franz Huning came to Albuquerque and became prosperous businessmen, contributing to Albuquerque's economic growth. Even before the arrival of the railroad, Albuquerque played an important role as a military outpost. The presence of troops created a demand for cattle, and ranching expanded to become an important industry with the arrival of the railroad. Santa Fe, however, maintained its territorial prominence because of its position as a trade center and its revenue from government agencies. Additionally, with the coming of the AT&SF in 1880, rail transportation facilitated expansion into the territory and Albuquerque's central location established the town as a gateway to surrounding areas. Importantly, Albuquerque had direct access to the railroad, whereas Santa Fe relied on the eighteen-mile spur, with rail traffic only twice a day.[5]

C. M. Chase, editor of the *Vermont Union*, had this to say about Albuquerque in 1882:

> The old town of Albuquerque is a mile from the depot, and
> like all other Mexican towns, is built of adobe, one story flat
> top houses, and for years has been the headquarters of many
> rich Mexican traders and stock raisers. The new town, of
> course, starts from the depot and works toward the old
> town.... A resident of a New England town, stationary in its
> business methods, society resources, productions, etc, can
> scarcely appreciate the hurry, confusion, the anxiety, the fuss
> and the hum-drum, incident to one of those new western
> towns, growing rapidly into the impetus of the town rivalry
> and great expectations.
>
> Albuquerque claims future importance on the strength of
> being a railroad center, of being located in a central position in
> the Territory, of having some mineral wealth, now being
> worked and to be developed, of having the trade of the Navajo
> Indian stock raisers on the east. But her best claim is based on
> the strength of the railroads. The Atlantic and Pacific intersects
> here with the Atchison, Topeka, and the Santa Fe and the
> repair shops and round houses of that company are in the
> process of erection....
>
> Last February, in the locality of the depot there was noth-
> ing but two or three shanties and a few cloth tents. But a town
> was among the certainties of the future, and lots were selling
> for $100. Today, it would be difficult to count the business
> houses. The growth has surprised everyone.[6]

The Atchison, Topeka, and Santa Fe line ran two miles east of the plaza where a "New Town" soon emerged.[7] A line of horse-drawn vehicles was used to link the two towns.[8] The architecture of the new town differed from the traditional architecture of Old Town, which, like Santa Fe, reflected both Native American and Spanish influence. With the advantage of rail transportation into the new town came eastern and European influences in architecture. Materials were easily transported on rail cars, and the new town grew quickly. Albuquerque businessmen saw

The Town Down the Tracks

Figure 25: Hope's European Hotel and Restaurant, 1885 (Railroad Ave., now Central Ave.). Courtesy of the Museum of New Mexico, neg. no. 76060.

the possible profits to be earned by railroad access to their city and began to buy up land. A new real estate firm, New Mexico Town Company, headed by Franz Huning, William C. Hazeldine, Elias S. Stover, and officers of the railroad, acquired land for the Atchison, Topeka, and Santa Fe.[9] The new company bought several large parcels of land and deeded them to the AT&SF for one dollar; in return, the proprietors were to receive one-half of the net profit from the land sales in the new town.[10] Huning made immense profits on his investment of town lots and benefited greatly from the proximity of the railroad to his mill.[11] Roads were laid out in grid form running parallel of the tracks. The new thoroughfare, Railroad Avenue (later to be renamed Central Avenue) intersected with First Street, most commonly referred to then as Front Street, which ran directly in front of the tracks.[12] Subdivisions and commercial business started to expand along the tracks a mile or so east of the original Old Town. The new town would eventually grow to encompass Old Town and later develop to become the largest city in the state. With the railroad's main line coming through Albuquerque, Santa Fe lagged economically, while Albuquerque prospered.[13]

At one point in the early 1900s, Albuquerqueans petitioned the legislature to build a new capital in their town. Santa Feans fought the bill

Figure 26: First Street Looking North, 1885. Gift from Mr. and Mrs. Mickey Miller. Courtesy of the Albuquerque Museum Photoarchives, PA1980.152.2.

vigilantly, spending many thousands of dollars to defeat the ambitious and grasping community sixty miles to the south.[14] Although Albuquerque had won out over Santa Fe and Las Vegas to establish a territorial university, Santa Fe remained the political center of New Mexico.[15]

Framed structures began to appear after the arrival of the railroad, and construction with brick and native stone held a sharp contrast to the adobe structures of Old Town and Santa Fe.[16] The new look of American modernity did not offer the comfort of the traditional adobe homes that remained cool in the summer and held the heat in the winter. Yet the construction of these more modern structures gained popularity among newcomers from the East as a transition to Americanizing the Southwest and also positioned Albuquerque ahead of Santa Fe as an emerging modern city. In contrast, Santa Fe kept its Spanish architecture with all of its charm and quaintness, leaving it in a class by itself, and attracting curious visitors from around the world. Isaac H. Rapp was responsible for creating the standards for Santa Fe Style, the City Different. He commissioned over fifteen building projects in Santa Fe, and in several other towns throughout the region, but never in Albuquerque.[17] Although

The Town Down the Tracks

Figure 27: Barnett Building, 1896. Photographer: Walton. Gift of Glen Schwegemann. Courtesy of the Albuquerque Museum Photoarchives, PA1978.77.31.

Albuquerque's Old Town strived to retain much of its historical quaintness (and to this day Old Town Plaza holds this classic charm), the dominance of this architectural style in Santa Fe placed the capital in a class distinctly different from other architecturally modern towns and cities along the tracks.

The Atchison, Topeka, and Santa Fe acquired a large tract of land for a depot and rail yards within the city limits of New Town, and was the largest property owner in the city. Because Santa Fe had no rail yard, Albuquerque prospered as a railway headquarters and became the main terminal between Los Angeles, California, and Topeka, Kansas.[18] The rail yard employed a large force of people and helped to boost the city's economy. The closing of the Santa Fe Trail as a conduit for trade with Santa Fe had led to a decline in the city's population. In 1890 the census for Santa Fe recorded 6,185 residents to Albuquerque's 3,785.[19] By 1900 the population of Santa Fe had dropped to 5,603, whereas Albuquerque's increased to 6,238. By 1910 Albuquerque's population was twice that of Santa Fe's, with roughly 11,020 people as opposed to just 5,072 in Santa Fe.[20] With the introduction of the railroad, Albuquerque emerged over

Santa Fe as "the metropolis of New Mexico," but the promotional campaigns led by the Atchison, Topeka, and Santa Fe Railroad would later pull Santa Fe above Albuquerque as a visitor destination for those who wished to experience the many facets of a historical Southwestern town.[21]

Before the turn of the century, New Town Albuquerque had encountered its own growing pains, as the streets became a hodgepodge of bars, gambling houses, and "palaces of forbidden pleasure."[22] Railroad workers with their paychecks subsidized saloonkeepers and gamblers, as well as ladies of ill repute. While the population of Santa Fe remained stable, with a majority of local Hispanics, New Town Albuquerque along the tracks grew with incoming Anglos from the East and other areas of the United States. By the early 1900s, Albuquerqueans realized that in order to gain statehood they needed to clean up their own town and elevate it to greater respectability among other aspiring Southwestern towns. On the other hand, Santa Fe's political position in the territory helped it sustain a more law-abiding citizenry. Relatively isolated by the eighteen-mile rail spur from Lamy, Santa Fe did not have to contend with a population of rail workers who demanded entertainment opportunities of questionable morality. The Atchison, Topeka, and Santa Fe itself recognized that Albuquerque needed respectable lodging facilities for its weary passengers as well as a genteel venue for its city's god-fearing residents.

In 1901 the Santa Fe Railroad began construction of a showcase hotel in Albuquerque. Like La Fonda in Santa Fe, the Fred Harvey Company ran the Alvarado Hotel, including its adjoining restaurant and shops.[23] A brochure published by the Santa Fe Railroad touted Albuquerque as:

> The largest city in the territory... where the Santa Fe has a
> grand division and three local divisions, and shops, a hospital,
> tie treating plant, and a splendid Harvey hotel (the Alvarado):
> and where local capital has established many jobbing houses
> and a number of manufacturing institutions.[24]

The same publication claimed that Albuquerque was "the largest and most industrious city on the line of the Santa Fe Railway between Los Angeles and Denver."[25]

The number of hotels in Albuquerque soon outnumbered those in Santa Fe. This was due to Albuquerque's new status as an industry and

Figure 28: Alvarado Hotel, ca. 1904–7. Courtesy of the Museum of New Mexico, neg. no. 14563.

Figure 29: Alvarado Hotel, ca. 1905. Photograph by G. W. Hance (Santa Fe Railway). Courtesy of the Museum of New Mexico, neg. no. 66003.

Figure 30: Alvarado Hotel Postcard. Courtesy of the Museum of New Mexico, neg. no. 40315.

trade center. By 1909–1910, Albuquerque offered visitors twenty hotels to choose from, compared to only four in Santa Fe.[26] Albuquerque also had four curio shops, whereas Santa Fe had only three.[27] The marketing of Indian handcrafts, fostered by the Indian Detours campaign, soon would change this, and Santa Fe would outrank Albuquerque both in the production of local mementos and in the number of souvenir shops.

After 1904, Harvey's Alvarado Hotel represented Albuquerque's premier hotel. Built according to the Southwestern Revival style, which combined the Native American and Spanish Colonial styles of architecture (the latter is perhaps best represented today by the California missions), it was constructed under the supervision of Charles P. Whittesey, the chief architect for the Santa Fe Railroad.[28] Also participating in this project was Mary Colter, whose style of interior décor would be evident in the renovation of La Fonda Hotel in the later 1920s, at the initiation of the Indian Detours campaign. Indeed, her forty-year career, which would culminate in the formulation of a popular regional style for the Southwest, got its start in 1902 when she went to work for Harvey and the AT&SF by decorating the interior of

The Town Down the Tracks

Figure 31: Indian Room—Alvarado Hotel, 1905. Photograph by Hance and Mast. Courtesy of the Museum of New Mexico, neg. no. 1507.

the Alvarado Hotel. The new hostelry included a restaurant, barber-shop, reading room, and seventy-five rooms, of which twenty had baths. Native rugs, handcrafted baskets, and pottery embellished the lobby, dining room, and hallways. The hotel's museum and sales room for Indian handcrafts featured local Pueblo artists and collectors items.[29] In 1913, Harvey added a western building, another curio room, and a newsstand to the museum area. By 1922 the Alvarado was expanded to become the largest Harvey Hotel. During the Depression, when most Harvey Houses closed, the establishments in the Southwest, including both the Alvarado and La Fonda, remained open and for the most part busy.[30] The Alvarado would celebrate its fiftieth anniversary, but by the 1970s it was torn down to make way for facilities with more modern amenities.[31] Through all of this, however, La Fonda, which was once at the heart of the AT&SF's most prestigious Southwestern campaign, Indian Detours, continued to entice countless visitors into its lobby for a peek at its historic quaintness and Southwestern décor; this décor remains an important ingredient of the hotel's charm.[32]

Selling Albuquerque, the AT&SF Way

The railroad attempted to entice visitors to Albuquerque in much the same way it had for Santa Fe. Yet, because of Albuquerque's growing identity as a commercial center, it was advertised in a somewhat different light. The 1924 edition of *Old-New Santa Fe and Roundabout* included a section on "Motor and Camping Trips from Albuquerque" led by Koshare Tours, which first contracted with the AT&SF but later was bought out by the rail-road.[33] A rail traveler could choose any of six one- to three-day trips. These included trips to Taos, Isleta, Jemez, or Ácoma, and were designed to

> bring the traveler in contact with old legends, folk dances, and weird dramatic ceremonies: prehistoric ruins, Indian pueblos, old missions, ranches and trading posts, quaint old towns and modern art colonies; mountains, canyons, forests, trout streams, mineral wells, salt lakes, lava flows, volcanoes, lofty buttes, sand-carvings and mesas.[34]

Tour guides made a point of escorting parties to specific Indian dances and fiestas and other interesting sites "off the beaten path." Whereas most trips from Albuquerque included a stay of at least one night, Santa Fe offered several one-day trips to interesting places and events in close proximity to the city. Geographically, both Santa Fe and Albuquerque are situated in valleys with mountains skirting the town's borders. The 1928 brochure *off the beaten path in the Great Southwest* described Albuquerque as "flanked by the hidden beauty of the Sandia and Jemez Mountains. The climate, somewhat warmer than that of Santa Fe, is clear and sunny and famed for its year-around healthfulness."[35] Promotional materials for both towns touted their clear, dry, crisp air as ideal for those who suffered from lung problems.

By the 1950s the Santa Fe Railroad and the Fred Harvey Company expanded their promotional campaigns to attract auto and air passengers. In 1956, a one-page ad appeared in the 250th anniversary issue of *Enchantarama of Albuquerque*. Bold letters across the top stated, "It started as a Diversion . . ."; the article summarized Fred Harvey's beginning in Albuquerque:

> Thus Fred Harvey introduced himself to the town. He had become deeply interested in the products of the Southwest and

Figure 32: Zuni Guide and Young Traveler, n.d. Photograph by Santa Fe Railway. Courtesy of the Museum of New Mexico, neg. no. 183129.

recognized their importance for the travel trade. For many a traveler "just passing through" decided that the land creating such fascinating things might be worth a visit.... Travelers wanting to stay must have a place to stay. In 1901, Fred Harvey opened the new Alvarado Hotel next to its Indian Building. . . . When Albuquerque expanded to the foothills of the Sandias, their canyons began to echo the roar of airplanes. In 1948, the Fred Harvey Company, now grown to "3000 Miles of Hospitality" took over the restaurants in the new Municipal Airport. They are known to travelers and townspeople as good places to eat—and, although modern they are distinctly Fred Harvey.[36]

The last page of the pamphlet included a full-page announcement from the AT&SF on the "new Luxury Service for Coach-Fare Travel" from Chicago to Los Angeles, highlighting the "New 'Hi-Level' El Capitan."

Santa Fe continued to advertise both Albuquerque and Santa Fe in the 1958 promotional campaign, *Along the Route.* The town of Santa Fe with its old San Miguel Church is highlighted in the New Mexico section, whereas Albuquerque follows two pages later. The article states that Albuquerque was the site of a military outpost during Spanish and Mexican occupation and was "second only in importance to Santa Fe."[37] The pamphlet tells the reader that the "Altitude, sunshine and low humidity make this a good place for treating pulmonary troubles out of doors" and expounds on the town as a cultural and educational center that included the sixty-acre campus of the University of New Mexico.[38] Like Santa Fe, the railroad company highlighted Albuquerque's history, architecture, and arid healthy environment, but the town never achieved Santa Fe's fame as a Southwestern tourist destination.

Heath Seekers and Albuquerque

Albuquerque gradually gained recognition as a health seeker's destination. By the late 1890s, the Atchison, Topeka, and Santa Fe campaigned through leaflets and pamphlets on the health benefits that both Albuquerque and Santa Fe provided, yet it appears that the railroad preferred Santa Fe over Albuquerque. In 1895, one of the railroad's brochures, *The New Southwest,* boasted the benefits of Santa Fe's "dry, equable, sunny climate," but neglected to advertise Albuquerque as a health destination. Two years later, the Passenger Department of the Santa Fe Route published *New Mexico Health Resorts,* which included climate, elevation, and lodging information on both towns. The brochure

The Town Down the Tracks

noted that Albuquerque had no sanatoriums and that "those needing the special treatment and care only afforded in such institutions must look elsewhere."[39] The same brochure advertised St. Vincent's Sanatorium and other professional services available in Santa Fe. While this pamphlet contained one and one-half pages on a description of Albuquerque and the amenities that could be found there for health seekers, the section on Santa Fe was over four pages long. A companion piece to this was produced that listed the principal health and pleasure resorts from New Mexico, Colorado, Arizona, and California. Accommodations at one of Albuquerque's featured hotels were listed at fifty cents to one dollar a day, and rooms at boarding houses for eight to twelve dollars a week. Similar accommodations in Santa Fe were more expensive; hotels ranged from $1.50 to $3.00 per day (at the Palace Hotel), or $9.00 to $10.00 a week.[40]

By the end of the century New Mexico became a haven for those suffering from the "White Plague" (tuberculosis), and the territory grew to be known as "nature's sanatorium for consumptives."[41] New Mexico gained national recognition in 1908 by ranking fifth in the nation in the number of facilities for tuberculosis patients.[42] By 1912 the number of doctors had more than doubled over the numbers just ten years earlier.[43] As New Mexico Territory became increasingly "modernized" with the encroachment of migrants firm the East, doctors found the area an attractive and enticing place to set up practice.

Along with the railroad, the Albuquerque Civic Council also led a successful campaign to highlight the city's climate.[44] In 1915, the Chamber of Commerce coined a new phrase for Albuquerque: "where the sick get well and the well get prosperous!"[45] Albuquerque ranked with towns such as Denver, San Antonio, San Diego, and Los Angeles as chief resort cities; Phoenix and Tucson did not hit the list until much later, possibly reflecting the underdevelopment of rail lines in Arizona.[46] On the eve of World War I, close to 50 percent of the Albuquerque population consisted of victims of tuberculosis and their family members.[47] Like Santa Fe, Albuquerque's clinics and sanitariums catered to tuberculosis patients and asthmatics who were "chasing the cure."[48] By the late 1920s Albuquerque's main sources of income were the Santa Fe Railroad and the tuberculosis trade.[49] While the railroad appeared to favor Santa Fe's facilities as a health resort over Albuquerque's, both Santa Fe and Albuquerque prospered as health destinations.

Art, Artists, and Albuquerque

Albuquerque never acquired a reputation as an artist community in the manner that Santa Fe had in the 1900s. Like Santa Fe, however, Albuquerque had several venues to showcase Southwestern art. The Indian Room at the Albuquerque Depot offered many travelers their first glimpse of Southwestern handcrafts, and Native Americans were allowed to peddle their crafts to passengers along the rail. Train passengers had the opportunity to stretch their legs and venture through the streets of downtown Albuquerque in hopes of finding a treasure from the "Sunshine State."

In the early 1900s Santa Fe had more curio shops than Albuquerque. This likely was fostered by the railroad's advertisement of Santa Fe as an artist's destination and by the Indian Detours campaign that highlighted Native American culture. Santa Fe continued to lead Albuquerque in the number of curio shops until the 1950s.[50] Even then, however, Santa Fe continued to surpass Albuquerque in number of shops per capita, and it has never fallen behind.[51] As early as the 1920s, Santa Fe artists opened galleries to entice travelers to venture into their studios, in hopes that they would purchase a piece of work. Much later, in the 1990s, The Albuquerque Convention and Visitor's Bureau launched large campaigns to showcase the "Art of Albuquerque." This campaign featured the work of several artists on panels affixed to buses from the Albuquerque Sun Trans public-transportation system. Today a number of galleries are scattered throughout Albuquerque, with a concentration in Old Town. Most of these shops feature local and state artists in a variety of media including "old pawn" jewelry.[52] Similar materials can also be found in the area of Santa Fe's Plaza and on the famous Canyon Road.[53]

In their efforts to use the Albuquerque train depot as a venue to display New Mexican art, it was the artwork of Santa Fe artists, in the early advertising campaigns of the Atchison, Topeka, and Santa Fe that fostered Santa Fe's dominant position as an artist's community and marketplace, a position it still holds.

Competitive Advertising and Contemporary Albuquerque

As the automobile became the preferred mode of transportation in the 1950s, Route 66 became the lifeline to the city. This transcontinental

The Town Down the Tracks

highway was literally Albuquerque's main street, Central Avenue. The automobile age eventually changed Albuquerque, which evolved from a community with thoroughfares in the heart of the city to an interstate network, which completely bypassed congested areas, including downtown. As with other burgeoning cities, Albuquerque also witnessed emergent suburban shopping centers that drew consumers away from the once-flourishing downtown area. Additionally, downtown Albuquerque failed to retain some of its historic tourist attractions. A major blunder of Albuquerqueans was allowing the demolition of some of the city's great landmarks, especially the Franciscan Hotel in the 1950s and the Alvarado Hotel in 1970. At one point, Albuquerque struggled to revive its moribund downtown area.[54] Since the 1990s civic groups have initiated several efforts to revitalize the downtown area. Albuquerque's downtown district, however, with its tall business buildings and contrasting modern and historic architecture, Old Town, and University of New Mexico area, remains a popular place to visit.

In an informal interview in 2003, Mary Kay Cline, president of the Albuquerque Convention and Visitors Bureau (and considered by many to be "New Mexico's First Lady of Tourism"), was asked how her organization is currently marketing the city.[55] She answered that the city's promotional campaigns likely were doing the same things they did forty years ago. She acknowledged that Santa Fe long promoted its distinct ethnic. Albuquerque, on the other hand, has evolved . . . from a small settlement to a city, and finally to a major metropolitan area with considerable commercial appeal. Its selling points continue to be the climate, the friendly atmosphere, and the topography. Over the last twenty-five years of Cline's involvement with Albuquerque's hospitality industry, she has seen the addition of more museums, cultural centers, and "sophisticated" entertainment. This is where, she adds, Albuquerque has become more eclectic than Santa Fe. The "cachet" of Santa Fe and its attraction to visitors is its movie stars, the architecture, the food, and the culture. Albuquerque is an authentic destination—organic in nature—that has evolved with the times. Additionally, Albuquerque provides a larger variety of accommodations for travelers, in price ranges and physical amenities, than Santa Fe.

While zoning laws in Santa Fe restricted growth, Albuquerque's city leaders planned the development of their community, making

Albuquerque one of the most sprawling cities in the West. Whereas Albuquerque grew as a business-friendly city that promoted commercial and economic opportunity, Santa Fe reflected a slow-paced, regional life style (as well as being environmentally sensitive).

For the period 1999–2001, the Albuquerque area dominated the Santa Fe area in terms of lodgers' tax revenues (a reflection of hotel occupancy rate).[56] These numbers reflect Albuquerque's role as a military base (Kirtland Air Force Base), a scientific laboratory (Sandia Labs), and a technology center (Intel). In addition, Albuquerque hosts the Annual Albuquerque International Balloon Fiesta, which attracts three quarters of a million to one million visitors each fall. For the summer tourist season, however, the Santa Fe area ranked highest in the entire state for lodgers' tax revenues. For the 2001 summer season, Santa Fe County attracted $1,972,518, whereas Bernalillo County attracted only $1,395,796 in lodgers' tax.[57]

Southwestern historian Marc Simmons believes that, similar to Santa Fe, Albuquerque's growth and success is tied closely to the railroad. Albuquerque won out for the main line over Santa Fe largely because of its spirit of "boosterism."[58] On the other hand, Santa Fe did not have room to grow and was considered too quaint. Incoming residents from Kansas started from scratch to redesign "New Town" Albuquerque in the image of their home state; many wanted their Queen Anne style houses, similar to what they had in the Midwest. Furthermore, in the late 1800s, many newcomers believed Santa Fe and its politics to be "backwards and tainted."[59] As Simmons noted, there is no question that Albuquerque holds the position of economic dominance in New Mexico. Santa Fe, however, has maintained its quaintness and charm over the decades, and this continues to draw visitors from all over the world to experience its history, culture, and architecture. Albuquerque may be the "gateway to enchantment," but Santa Fe *is* "the city different."

THE AT&SF'S LINGERING EFFECTS ON TOURISM IN MODERN DAY SANTA FE

The AT&SF promoted the many facets that define Santa Fe as a tourist's destination. The railroad highlighted one such feature, the cultures of the Santa Fe area, in a variety of ways to encourage and promote passenger travel to Santa Fe. Since the coming of the railway, the cultures of the Santa Fe area have been "on display" for numerous curious visitors. Santa Fe continues to be recognized for its tricultural identity, and the Santa Fe Chamber of Commerce and Visitors Bureau continue to use this feature as a means to market what they refer to as the "City Different."[1]

In the early guidebooks published by the AT&SF, the Pueblo people were referred to as "savage" or "wild," and the AT&SF continued to portray Native Americans as "living relics" of a culture that continued and sometimes struggled to hold on to its ancient religious beliefs and notions of tradition.[2] The railroad used the "primitive" to sell Santa Fe as a cultural destination.[3] In *Imagining Indians in the Southwest*, Dilworth provides an excellent example of the definition of primitivism and how it helped to define the Southwest. She believes that primitivism played a major role in shaping the Southwest as a distinct cultural region because the area was "known as a place of the unique handmade, the rural, and the authentic, as opposed to the modern metropolis, which was characterized as a place of mass produced objects and culture, the urban and the spurious."[4]

Several employees of the Atchison, Topeka, and Santa Fe preserved this romantic concept of Native American culture.[5] Perhaps most apparent among these were W. H Simpson, Rodger W. Birdseye from the Advertising Department, and Herman Schweizer from the Indian Department. Simpson, the advertising executive mentioned earlier, embellished and magnified many aspects of Pueblo culture during his thirty-three years of service. He worked with Santa Fe artists to follow a style that created a popular idealistic image of the cultures of Southwest, with Santa Fe as its cultural corridor. Reproductions of these images often were found on the pages of brochures that promoted the town of Santa Fe.[6] The Atchison, Topeka, and Santa Fe also used this "culture on canvas" to sell the Santa Fe area as a tourist destination by displaying the original works in Santa Fe depots throughout the country.[7]

Additionally, the brochures provided descriptions of the cultures found in Santa Fe. *Off the Beaten Path in the Great Southwest* told readers who stayed at La Fonda that they could catch "intimate glimpses of Indian life not otherwise obtainable."[8] A 1935 railroad brochure about the Santa Fe area claimed that "colonial Spain lives on through the sunny centuries, dominating life, language and architecture of the in-numerable communities."[9] Many of the images used in the Santa Fe Railroad brochures followed the descriptions used by famous writers such as Charles Lummis and Zane Grey.[10] These two writers also brought the distinct cultures in and around Santa Fe to life in novels, as did other authors who contributed works of fiction that embellished the Indian and Hispanic cultures of the Southwest.[11] The Harvey Newsstand in La Fonda promoted and sold many of these works of fiction.[12] Santa Fe continues to draw popular authors to write about the area's cultural distinctiveness. Richard Bradford's *Red Sky at Morning*, John Nichols's *The Milagro Beanfield War*, and Jo-Ann Mapson's *Blue Rodeo* are but a few of the works that relate the charm of Santa Fe and the Sangre de Cristo Mountains, which dominate the northeastern skyline of the city.[13]

The Indian Detours sightseeing company and promotional brochures highlighted the cultures around Santa Fe in a nationwide advertising campaign. A 1929 article in *The Santa Fe Magazine* claimed that in Santa Fe "the enduring impression of the Spanish padres and the conquistadors is everywhere. The life of the Indian, the Spanish American and frontier Southwest runs side by side."[14] The tour service provided visitors with an intimate perspective of the daily lives of the local people. Today ritual dances, powwows, and feast days are held at the Pueblos around Santa Fe and often are open to the public.[15] Although photography or sketching of many events often is prohibited, several Pueblos charge a photo fee to those visitors who wish to record what they may perceive as an unchanging culture.[16] Today, the Santa Fe Convention and Visitors Bureau Visitor Guide promotes the cultures of Santa Fe by informing its readers how "Santa Fe is enriched by the vital, living traditions of the many distinctive cultures that call it home."[17]

As the cultures mixed and evolved so did the area's architecture. Mud houses slowly transformed to a more weather-resistant image of the Pueblo Revival or Territorial style, creating what became known as Santa Fe Style. This emphasis on architectural uniqueness inspired "the regionalism movement in the arts... in the late twenties and thirties," which continues to be the feature that sets this city apart from all other Southwestern destinations.[18] This style is showcased in La Fonda, which maintains a dominant position on the Plaza's southeast corner, across from the Governor's Palace.

Santa Fe has sustained its popularity as a nationally recognized tourist destination, thanks to the foundation laid by the promotional efforts of the Santa Fe Railroad. The popular international travel magazine *Condé Nast Traveler* surveys its readers annually to ascertain the "hot" vacation destinations in the United States. Santa Fe maintained its fourth-place rating for both 1999 and 2000 (exceeded only by San Francisco, New Orleans, and Charleston) making it the top destination in the American Southwest.[19] By 2003, Santa Fe fell to fifth place with Chicago sneaking into fourth, yet the *Travel and Leisure* poll placed the Southwestern town in third place surpassed only by New York and San Francisco.[20]

The Santa Fe Railroad blazed new trails in promoting the architecture, scenery, and cultures in and around its namesake town. The methods employed by this company to spotlight the ethnic cultures, the unique architecture, the comfortable climate, and the breathtaking beauty of the Southwest were intended to leave a dynamic residue and add a cachet of glamour to the eye of the visitor. This sense of historical authenticity continues to lure people to this unusual enchanted destination, offering them a glimpse of native New Mexicans and their daily lives. Thus, the transformation of the country's oldest capital from a small remote Southwest town to the foremost destination of the Southwest was carefully and painstakingly scripted by the railroad system that bore the town's name. Much of our contemporary perception and experience of Santa Fe can be traced directly or indirectly to the marketing efforts of the Atchison, Topeka, and Santa Fe Railroad system, in its efforts to capitalize on the mystic and allure of the City Different.

BROCHURES BY THE AT&SF AND THE FRED HARVEY COMPANY

The publications listed below were produced by the Santa Fe Railway System and/or the Fred Harvey Company and included promotional advertising or information on Santa Fe, New Mexico. Some publications include print-run figures at the end of the citation. Please note, however, this is not an inclusive list.

1891
New Mexico: A Land of Prosperity and Happiness. Chicago: Rand McNally & Co., 1891.

1895
The New Southwest: New Mexico Rio Grande Valley, Arizona Salt River Valley. Chicago: Rand, McNally & Co., circa 1895.

1897
New Mexico Health Resorts. Passenger Department Santa Fe Route, 1897.

1898
Resorts on the Santa Fe. Passenger Department Santa Fe Route, 1898.

1900
Climatology and Mineral Springs of New Mexico—Health and Pleasure Resorts. Santa Fe: New Mexico Printing Company, 1900. Photos Courtesy of The Santa Fe Route.

1903
Dorsey, George A., Ph.D. *Indians of the Southwest.* Passenger Department of the AT&SF Railway System, February 1903.
Higgins, C. A. *To California Over the Santa Fe Trail.* Chicago: Passenger Department, The Santa Fe, August 1903.

1904

The Camera in the Southwest. Kansas City: Fred Harvey, 1904.

1910

Free Lands and Dry Farming in the Southwest. Issued by General
    Colonization Department, Atchison, Topeka and Santa Fe
    Railway, Chicago: Blakely-Oswald Printing Co., July 1910. 5M.
New Mexico. Chicago: Poole Bros., September 1910. 10M.

1911

The Great Southwest Along the Santa Fe. Kansas City: Fred Harvey, 1911.

1912

Santa Fe de-Luxe. Chicago: Newman-Monroe Co., September 1912.
Old-New Santa Fe and Roundabout. Chicago: Press of the Henry O.
    Shepard Co., 1912.

1913

New Mexico: The Sunshine State. Published by Colonization Department,
    AT&SF Railway. Chicago: Henry O. Shepard Co., March 1913.

1914

The Great Southwest Along the Santa Fe. Kansas City: Fred Harvey, 1914.
Santa Fe de-Luxe. Chicago: Poole Bros., 1914. 20M.

1916

Old-New Santa Fe and Roundabout. Chicago: Press of the Henry O.
    Shepard Co., May 1916. 15M.

1917

Higgins, C. A., *To California Over the Santa Fe Trail,* Chicago:
    Passenger Department, Santa Fe, 1917.
Off the Beaten Path in New Mexico and Arizona. Chicago: Press of the
    Henry O. Shepard Co., July 1917. 15M.
New Mexico: The Sunshine State. Published by Industrial Department,
    AT&SF Railway. Chicago: Henry O. Shepard Co., September

Brochures by the AT&SF

1917. 5M.

1919

The Great Southwest Along the Santa Fe. Kansas City: Fred Harvey,
    1919. (See 1911.)

1921

The Great Southwest Along the Santa Fe. 70th thousand. 6th ed. of
    1911c. Kansas City: Fred Harvey, 1921.
"La Fonda" At the End of the Santa Fe Trail. N.p., circa 1921.

1923

The Great Southwest Along the Santa Fe. 85th thousand. 7th ed. of 1911c.
    Kansas City: Fred Harvey, 1923.
Old-New Santa Fe and Roundabout. Chicago: Hedstrom-Barry Co.
    Printers, May 1923. Intro. by Chas F. Lummis. 20M.

1924

Old-New Santa Fe and Roundabout. Chicago: Hedstrom-Barry Co.
    Printers, June 1924. Intro. by Chas F. Lummis. 20M.

1925

Old-New Santa Fe and Roundabout. Chicago: Hedstrom-Barry Co.
    Printers, June 1925. Intro. by Chas F. Lummis. 20M.
The Great Southwest Along the Santa Fe. 93d thousand. 8th ed. of 1911c.
    Kansas City: Fred Harvey, 1925.
The Indian-detour. Chicago: Rand McNally and Co., 1925. 10M.

1926

*The Indian-detours Santa Fe Fred Harvey: Newest Way to See Oldest
    America.* Chicago: Newman-Monroe, 1930.
Indian-detour. Chicago: Rand McNally & Company, April 1926. 30M.
Roads to Yesterday: More Drives Out from Old Santa Fé. Chicago:
    Hedstrom-Barry Co. Printers, May 1926.
By the Way Santa Fé. Chicago: Rand McNally & Company, August
    1926. 45M.

1927

Roads to Yesterday: Motor Drives Out from Old Santa Fé. Chicago:
    Hedstrom-Barry Co. Printers, March 1927. 25M.
Indian-detour. Chicago: Rand McNally & Company, August 1927. 40M.

1928

Indian-detour. Chicago: Rand McNally & Co., June 1928. 25M.
Harveycar Motor Cruises off the beaten path in the Great Southwest.
    Chicago: Rand McNally & Co., October 1928. 25M.
They Know New Mexico: Intimate Sketches by Western Writers. Issued by
    Passenger Department, AT&SF Railway. Chicago: Rand
    McNally & Company, 1928.

1929

Harveycar Motor Cruises off the beaten path in the Great Southwest.
    Chicago: Rand McNally & Co., January 1929. 30M.
La Fonda in Old Santa Fé: The Inn at The End of the Trail. Rand
    McNally & Co., July 1929.
Indian-detour. Chicago: Rand McNally & Co., October 1929. 40M.
The Great Southwest Along the Santa Fe. 104th thousand. 10th ed. of
    1911c. Kansas City: Fred Harvey, 1929.

1930

Indian-detours: off the beaten path in the Great Southwest. August 1930.
    40M.
Indian-detours-Most distinctive Motor Cruise Service in the World.
    Chicago: Rand McNally, November 1930. 25M.
La Fonda in Old Santa Fé New Mexico: The Inn at the End of the Trail.
    Chicago: Rand McNally, circa 1930.

1931

Indian-detours: off the beaten path in the Great Southwest. November 1931.

1932

Courier Cars. Chicago: Santa Fe System Lines, September 1932.

1933

Announcement (leaflet to accompany other ticketing information

Brochures by the AT&SF

regarding the changes in ownership and rates for "Indian Detours"). Chicago: Rand McNally, 1933.

1935

Santa Fe: Dude Ranch Country. Chicago: R. H. Donnelley Deeptone and Sons Co., 1935. 25M.

Santa Fe Fiesta. Chicago: Passenger Traffic, Santa Fe System Lines, July 29, 1935.

1936

La Fonda: Santa Fe, New Mexico. Kansas City: Alco-Geavure Inc., 1936.

1940

Indian-Detours, roundabout Old Santa Fe New Mexico. Chicago: Rand McNally, March 1940. 25M.

1958

Along the Route. Chicago: Rand McNally, April 1958.

SANTA FE HOTEL LISTINGS, 1880 TO 1940

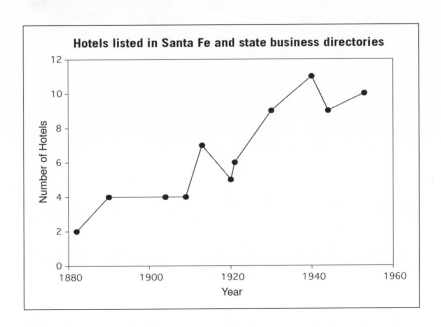

Hotels listed in Santa Fe and state business directories

1882 Exchange Hotel, Palace Hotel.

1883 Exchange Hotel, Herlow's Hotel, Palace Hotel (National Hotel was vacant).

1890 Alamo Hotel, Exchange Hotel, Palace Hotel, Prices Hotel.

1898 Claire Hotel, Exchange Hotel, Palace Hotel.

1904 Claire Hotel, Normandie, Palace Hotel, Sunmount.

1909 Claire Hotel, Coronado Hotel, Hotel Normandie, Palace Hotel.

1920 Bishop's Lodge, Capitol Hotel, Coronado Hotel, De Vargas Hotel, Montezuma Hotel.

1921 Bishop's Lodge, Capitol Hotel, Coronado Hotel, Doran Hotel, Hotel De Vargas, Montezuma Hotel.

1929* El Fidel Hotel, Hotel De Vargas, La Fonda, Montezuma Hotel, The Santa Fe Inn.

1930 Alvarado Hotel, Bishop's Lodge, Capitol Hotel, Coronado Hotel, Hotel De Vargas, El Fidel Hotel, Franciscan Hotel, La Fonda Hotel, Montezuma Hotel.

1940 Bishop's Lodge, Coronado Hotel, Hotel De Vargas, El Fidel Hotel, Franciscan Hotel, Hotel La Casa, La Fonda Hotel, La Posada, Montezuma Hotel, Plaza Hotel, Santa Fe Inn.

1944 Bishop's Lodge, Hotel De Vargas, El Fidel Hotel, Franciscan Hotel, Hotel La Casa, La Fonda Hotel, La Posada, Montezuma Hotel, Plaza Hotel.

1953 Bishop's Lodge, Hotel De Vargas, El Fidel Hotel, Fred Harvey Inc., Hope Hotel, Hotel La Casa, La Fonda Hotel, La Posada, Montezuma Hotel, Plaza Hotel.

Information for Appendix B was gathered from *Business Directory of New Mexico and Gazetteer of the Territory* (Santa Fe: New Mexico Printing and Publishing Co., 1882), 142. CSL, microfilm 549, reel 120; *Pointers on the Southwest* (Topeka: Sexton, 1883), 3. CSL microfilm 244; *Santa Fe, New Mexico* (Sanborn Map Company, 1882; 1886; 1890; 1898; 1902; 1908; 1913; 1913; 1921; 1930), CSL microfilm 242, reel 3; *New Mexico Business Directory For 1909–1910* (Denver: The Gazetteer Publishing Co., 1909), 880; *New Mexico State Business Directory 1920* (Denver: The Gazetteer Publishing Co., 1920), 605; *New Mexico State Business Directory 1921–1922* (Denver: The Gazetteer Publishing Co., 1921), 104–8; *New Mexico State Business Directory 1930* (Denver: The Gazetteer Publishing Co., 1930), 686; *Santa Fe City Directory 1944* (El

Santa Fe Hotel Listings, 1880 to 1940

Paso: Hudspeth Directory Co., 1944), 383; *Santa Fe City Directory 1953*
(El Paso: Hudspeth Directory Co., 1953), 372.

*Advertisements in *Santa Fe, New Mexico: The Ancient City*
(Santa Fe: Santa Fe Chamber of Commerce, 1929), Museum of New Mexico.

The directories were found at the Museum of New Mexico unless noted otherwise.

SANTA FE CURIO SHOP LISTINGS, 1900 TO 1940

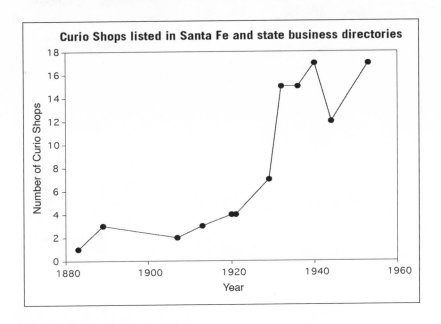

Curio Shops listed in Santa Fe and state business directories

1883   Jake Gold.

1889   Jake Gold, Thomas Moore, New Mexico Norfleet.

1907/8   J. S. Candelario, A. J. Spiegelberg.

1913/14 The Bradfields, J. S. Candelario, Juan Olivas.

1920   J. S. Candelario, J. F. Collins, Julius Gans, Juan Olivas.

1921   Candelario's Indian Trading Post, J. F. Collins Co., Juan Olivas, Southwest Arts and Crafts (owned by Julius Gans).

1929[*]   Burro Weavers, Emporium (Indian and Old Mexico Curio Dept.), Dick Marsh, McCrossen Hand-woven Products, Old Santa Fe Trading Post, Southwest Indian Trading Co., Spanish and Indian Trading, Inc.

1930/31   Abreu Marcus, Axtec Studio, Candelario's Indian Trading Post, J. F. Collins, La Fonda Indian Shop, Liane's, The Little Shop, Andrew Ohrn, Old Santa Fe Trading Post, Juan Olivas, San Miguel Curio Shop, Santa Fe Jewel Shop, Southwest Arts and Crafts, Spanish Arts, Spanish and Indian Trading Co., Thunder Bird Shop.

1932/33   Candelario's Indian Trading Post, J. F. Collins, Kraft Shop, La Fonda Indian Shop, Liane's, The Little Shop, Old Mexican Shop, Old Santa Fe Trading Post, San Miguel Curio Shop, Santa Fe Jewel Shop, Southwest Arts and Crafts, Spanish Arts, Spanish and Indian Trading Co., Thunder Bird Shop, Unique Jewelry Co.

1936/37   American Studio, Candelario's Indian Trading Post, La Fonda Indian Shop, The Little Shop, Native Market, Navajo Shop, Old Indian Shop, Old Santa Fe Trading Post, G. A. Ortiz, Southwest Arts and Crafts, Southwestern Master Craftsmen Inc., Spanish Chest, Spanish & Indian Trading Co., Thunder Bird Shop, Webb Young Trader.

1940   Cactus Shop, Candelario's Indian Trading Post, Chimayo Curio Store, La Fonda Indian Shop, Dick Marsh Indian Trader, Mission Bell, Native Market, Navajo Shop, Old Indian Shop, Old Mexico Shop, Old Santa Fe Trading Post, The Peasant Shop, Rios Tiburcio, Santa Fe Jewel Shop, Southwest Arts and Crafts, Southwestern Master Craftsmen Inc., Spanish and Indian Trading Co., Thunder Bird Shop.

1944   Candelario's Indian Trading Post, Chimayo Curio Shop, Dendahl's, La Fonda Indian Shop, Iris Card and Gift Shop, Navajo Shop, Old Mixico Shop, Old Santa Fe Trading Post,

Santa Fe Curio Shop Listings, 1900 to 1940

Peasant Shop, Frank Patania, Santa Fe Jewel Shop, Southwest Arts and Crafts, Southwestern Master Craftsmen Inc., Spritz Jewelry Store and Gift Shop, Thunder Bird Shop.

1953   Bedell Eleanor Trading Post, Chaparral Trading Post, Candelario's Indian Trading Post, Chimayo Curio Store, El Ortiz Curio Shop, La Fonda Indian Shop, Little Shop, Old Mexico Shop, Original Curio Shop, Quivira Indian Shop, Santa Fe Gift Shop, Shop of the Oldest House, Shop of the Rainbow Man, Southwest Arts and Crafts, Southwestern Master Craftsmen Inc., Spritz Jewelry Store and Gift Shop, Thunder Bird Shop.

Information for Appendix C was gathered from *McKenney's Business Directory* (Kansas City: Pacific Press, 1882), 339, Kansas State Historical Society; *Southern Pacific Coast Directory* (McKenney Directory Co, 1888), 480–87, CSL; *New Mexico Business Directory for 1903–04* (Denver: The Gazetteer Publishing Co., 1903), 634; *New Mexico Business Directory for 1907–08* (Denver: The Gazetteer Publishing Co., 1907), 803; *New Mexico Business Directory for 1913–14* (Denver: The Gazetteer Publishing Co., 1913), 819; *New Mexico Business Directory for 1913–14* (Denver: The Gazetteer Publishing Co., 1913), 819; *New Mexico Business Directory for 1920* (Denver: The Gazetteer Publishing Co., 1920), 561; *New Mexico Business Directory for 1921* (Denver: The Gazetteer Publishing Co., 1921), 102–12; *New Mexico Business Directory for 1930* (Denver: The Gazetteer Publishing Co., 1930), 629, Museum of New Mexico; *Santa Fe City Directory 1930–31* (El Paso: Hudspeth Directory Co., 1930), 260; *Santa Fe City Directory 1932–33* (El Paso: Hudspeth Directory Co., 1932), 223; *Santa Fe City Directory 1936–37* (El Paso: Hudspeth Directory Co., 1936), 276–77; *Santa Fe City Directory 1940* (El Paso: Hudspeth Directory Co., 1940), 354; *Santa Fe City Directory 1944* (El Paso: Hudspeth Directory Co., 1944), 372.

*Advertisements in *Santa Fe, New Mexico: The Ancient City* (Santa Fe: Santa Fe Chamber of Commerce, 1929).

The directories were found at the Museum of New Mexico unless noted otherwise.

POPULATION, ALBUQUERQUE AND SANTA FE

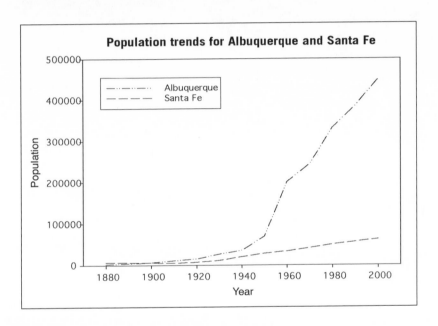

Population trends for Albuquerque and Santa Fe

DATE	1880	1890	1900	1910	1920	1930	1940	1950	1960	1970	1980	1990	2000
Santa Fe	6635	6185	5603	5072	7236	11179	20325	27998	33394	41167	49299	55859	62203
ABQ	2315	3785	6238	11020	15157	26570	35449	96815	201189	244501	332336	384736	448607

New Mexico Statistical Abstract (Albuquerque: University of New Mexico, Bureau of Business and Economic Research, 1989), 103, 106; *Ninth Census of the United States* (Washington, D.C.: U.S. Government Printing Office, 1871), v. 1, 206; *Fourteenth Census of the United States* (Washington, D.C.: U.S. Government Printing Office, 1921), v. 1, 529.

ALBUQUERQUE CURIO LISTINGS

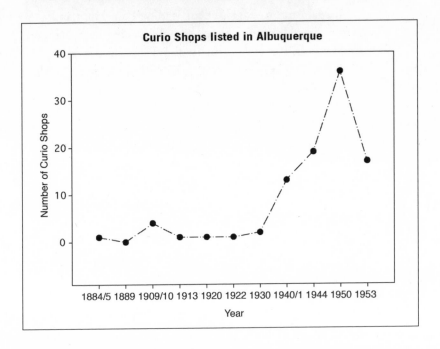

1882/83 Blain Bros. (Pawn Brokers).

1884/5 New Mexico Novelty Works.

1889 Nothing Listed.

1909/10 Bennett Curio Co., Indian and Mexican Building, Sam Kee, Chas. Wright.

1913/14 Ilfield Indian Trading Co., Wright's.

1920 Wright's Trading Post.

1922   Wright's Trading Post.

1930   Maisel's Indian Trading Post, Southwest Arts and Crafts, Thunderbird Shop.

1940/41 Ball Trading Post, Bell Trading Post, Curio Shop at the Municipal Airport, Eagle Indian Trading Post, Hunt and Davis, King's Turquoise Shop, Maisel's Trading Post, Navajo Trading Post, Parker's Indian Trading Post, Thunderbird Curio Store, War Bonnet, White Eagle Trading Post, Wright's Trading Post.

1944   Acoma Indian Curio Shop, Albuquerque Indian Sanatorium Gift Shop, Ball Trading Post, Bell Trading Post, Blue Sky Eagle Curios, Court Café Inc, Curio Shop at the Municipal Airport, Eagle Indian Trading Post, Fred Harvey Inc, Hilton Art and Curio Shop, King's Turquoise Shop, Maisel's Trading Post, Navajo Indian Store, Navajo Trading Post, Parker's Indian Trading Post, Powell Indian Trading Post, The Redman, Thunderbird Curio Store, War Bonnet, White Eagle Trading Post, Wright's Trading Post.

1950   Albuquerque Novelty Co., Alvarado New Stand, Bell Trading Post, Blue Eagle Trading Post, Casa Grande Curio, Covered Wagon, Crossed Arrows Trading Post, El Apache Trading Post, El Navajo Store, El Tombay Indian Shop, Franciscan Gift Shop, Hill Top Trading Post, Hunt's Trading Post, King's Curio and Gem Cutting, La Casa Del Tesoro, La Olaza Primoroso, La Tienda, Lobo Indian Store, Louie's Trading Post, Maisel's Indian Trading Post, New Mexicraft Co., Old Town Indian Trading Post, Omega's Originals, Osage Trading Post, Patio Pottery Shop, The Plaza Gallery, Ranchos Indian Store, Sedillo Trading Post, Seligman's Indian Craft, Star Indian Trading, Spector's Curio Store, Star Indian Trading Post, Thunderbird Curio Store, Tiquex Kiva Dolls, Tomahawk Trading Post, Torres Curio Store, Webb Indian Trading Post, White Eagle Trading Post, Whitfield's Curios,

Albuquerque Curio Listings

Wooden Indian, Wright's Trading Post.

1953   Al's Indian Shop, Apache Trading Post, Casa Chavela. Casa Grande Curio, Covered Wagon, El Tombay Indian Shop, Enchanted Mesa Trading Post, Fred Harvey Airport Curio Shop, Fred Harvey Curio and News Stand, Hunt's Trading Post, King's Curio and Gem Cutting, La Plaza Primorosa, La Tienda, Lobo Indian Store, Maisel's Indian Trading Post, Mexico-Curios, Old Town Indian Trading Post, Parker's Indian Trading Post, The Plaza, Rite Spot Curio, Seligman's Indian Craft, Star Indian Trading, Tomahawk Trading Post, Treasure House Plaza, Whitfield's Curios, Wright's Trading Post, Yei Be Chi Trading Post.

Information for Appendix E was gathered from *Albuquerque City Directory 1950* (El Paso: Hudspeth Directory Company, publisher, 1950), 124–26; *Albuquerque City Directory 1953* (El Paso: Hudspeth Directory Company, publisher, 1953), 24, 34; *Colorado, New Mexico, Utah, Nevada, Wyoming and Arizona Gazatteer and Business Directory* (Chicago: R. L. Polk and Co. and A. C. Danser, 1884), 306; *McKenney's Business Directory* (Kansas City: Pacific Press, 1882), 339, Kansas State Historical Society; *Southern Pacific Coast Directory* (McKenney Directory Co, 1888), 480–87, California State Library; *New Mexico Business Directory for 1903–04* (Denver: The Gazetteer Publishing Co., 1903), 634; *New Mexico Business Directory for 1907–08* (Denver: The Gazetteer Publishing Co., 1907), 803; *New Mexico Business Directory for 1909–10* (Denver: The Gazetteer Publishing Co., 1913), 852; *New Mexico Business Directory for 1920* (Denver: The Gazetteer Publishing Co., 1920), 561; *New Mexico Business Directory for 1922* (Denver: The Gazetteer Publishing Co., 1922), 541; *New Mexico Business Directory for 1930* (Denver: The Gazetteer Publishing Co., 1930), 688. *Southern Pacific Coast Directory; for 1888–9* (San Francisco: McKenney Directory Company, Publisher, April 1888).

*Advertisements in *Santa Fe, New Mexico: The Ancient City*
(Santa Fe: Santa Fe Chamber of Commerce, 1929).

The directories were found at the Museum of New Mexico unless noted otherwise.

ALBUQUERQUE HOTEL LISTINGS

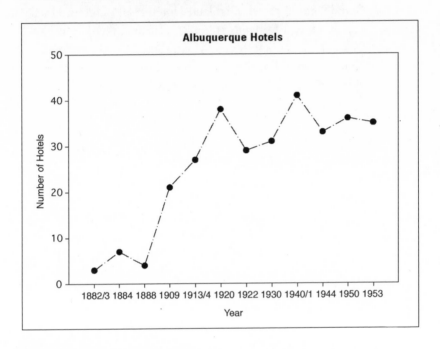

1882/03 Armijo Hotel, Hotel Maden, Journal Hotel.

1884/05 Alameda House, Albuquerque Hotel, Armijo House,
Exchange Hotel, Girard House, Hope's European Hotel,
Southern Hotel.

1888/09 Armijo House, Exchange Hotel, Girard House, Journal
Hotel, San Felipe Hotel, Windsor Hotel.

1909/10 Alvarado Hotel, Annex Hotel, Columbus Hotel, Commercial
Hotel, Denver Hotel, Geronimo Hotel, Grand Central Hotel,
Highland Hotel, Hotel Delaney, Metropolitan Hotel,
Minneapolis Hotel, Meyers Hotel, Oxford Hotel, Palace

Hotel, Savoy Hotel, Southern Hotel, St. Claire Hotel, Sturges Hotel, Vendome Hotel, Wayside Inn, Werner.

1913/14 Alvarado Hotel, American Hotel, Angelus Hotel, Annex Hotel, Club House Hotel, Commercial Hotel, Denver Hotel, Grand Central Hotel, Highland Hotel, Hotel Combs, Hotel Craige, Hotel Overland, Hotel Royal, Hotel Plymouth, Hotel Palace, Metropolitan Hotel, Montezuma Hotel, New State Hotel, Oxford Hotel, Palace Hotel, Savoy Hotel, Southern Hotel, St. Claire Hotel, Sturges Hotel, Vendome Hotel, Virginia Hotel, White House Hotel.

1920 Albuquerque Alamo Hotel, Albuquerque Hotel, Alvarado Hotel, American Hotel, Angelus Hotel, Annex Hotel, Atlantic Hotel, Bellevue Hotel, Bittner Hotel, Colombo Hotel, Commercial Hotel, Coronado Hotel, Dallas Hotel, Dodge Hotel, Elms Hotel, Gem Hotel, Gleason Hotel, Grand Central Hotel, Highland House, Highway Inn, Hotel Combs, Hotel Craige, Hotel Palace, Imperial Annex Hotel, Montezuma Hotel, New Albany Hotel, New State Hotel, Occidental Hotel, Rico Hotel, Savoy Hotel, State Hotel, Sturges Hotel, Sunnyside Inn, Superior Hotel, Tourist Hotel, Vendome Hotel.

1922 Albuquerque Alamo Hotel, Albuquerque Hotel, Alvarado Hotel, Angelus Hotel, Bellevue Hotel, Bittner Hotel, Bronx Hotel, Colombo Hotel, Coronado Hotel, Crystal Hotel, Elgin Hotel, Elms Hotel, Gem Hotel, Gleason Hotel, Grand Central Hotel, Combs, Hotel, Craige, Hotel Overland, Imperial Annex Hotel, Imperial Hotel, Linville Hotel, Montezuma Hotel, New State Hotel, Rico Hotel, Savoy Hotel, State Hotel, Sturges Hotel, Superior Hotel, Vendome Hotel.

1930 Albuquerque Airport Inn, Albuquerque Hotel, Alpine Hotel, Alvarado Hotel, Angelus Hotel, Atlantic Hotel, Bellevue Hotel, Bronx Hotel, Colombo Hotel, Combs Hotel, Coronado Hotel, Craige Hotel, Crystal Hotel, Elgin Hotel,

Albuquerque Hotel Listings

Elms Hotel, Franciscan, Grand Central Hotel, Henrietta Hotel, Hotel Clifton, Imperial Hotel, Montezuma Hotel, Occidental Hotel, Parenti Julia, Prairie Hotel, San Diego Hotel, Savoy Hotel, Sturges Hotel, Vendome Hotel, West Hotel, White House Hotel.

1940   Albuquerque Hotel, Alvarado Hotel, Angelus Hotel, Bronx Hotel, Combs Hotel, Courtesy Hotel, Craige Hotel, El Fidel Hotel, Elgin Hotel, Elms Hotel, Franciscan Hotel, Grand Central Hotel, Henrietta Hotel, Hilton Hotel, Howland Hotel, Hudson Hotel, Marion Hotel, Mayer Hotel, Milner Hotel, Occidental Hotel, Ranger Hotel, Redwing Hotel, Selvia Hotel, Sturges Hotel, Sun Hotel, Vendome Hotel.

1944   Albuquerque Hotel, Alpine Hotel, Alvarado Hotel, Angelus Hotel, Batchelor Hotel, Bellevue Hotel, Bronx Hotel, Combs Hotel, Courtesy Hotel, Craige Hotel, Economy Hotel, El Fidel Hotel, Elgin Hotel, Elms Hotel, Franciscan Hotel, Grand Central Hotel, Henrietta Hotel, Hilton Hotel, Howland Hotel, Hudson Hotel, Liberty Hotel, Marion Hotel, Massey Hotel, Mayer Hotel, Milner Hotel, Occidental Hotel, Palace Hotel, Ranger Hotel, Selvia Hotel, Sturges Hotel, Sun Hotel, Vendome Hotel, Vera Hotel.

1950   Alamo Hotel, Alvarado Hotel, Angelus Hotel, Batchelor Hotel, Casa Grande Lodge, Chicago Hotel, Courtesy Hotel, Craige Hotel, Downtown Hotel, El Fidel Hotel, Elgin Hotel, Elms Hotel, Franciscan Hotel, Grand Central Hotel, Henrietta Hotel, Hilton Hotel, Howland Hotel, Hudson Hotel, Ideal Hotel, Kings Hotel, Kipling Tourist Hotel, Liberty Hotel, Manhattan Hotel, Marion Hotel, Milner Hotel, New Mexican Hotel, Occidental Hotel, Palace Hotel, Park Inn Hotel, Ranger Hotel, Rio Grande Hotel, Sandia Hotel, Selvia Hotel, Sturges Hotel, Tucker Inn, Vera Hotel.

Information for Appendix F was gathered from *Albuquerque City Directory 1940* (El Paso: Hudspeth Directory Company, publisher, 1940),

705; *Classified Buyers' Guide of the City of Albuquerque 1944* (El Paso: Hudspeth Directory Company, publisher, 1944), 734; *Colorado, New Mexico, Utah, Nevada, Wyoming and Arizona Gazatteer and Business Directory* Chicago: R. L. Polk and Co. and A. C. Danser, 1884), 298–308; *McKienney's Business Directory* (Oakland: Pacific Press Publishers, 1882), 330–33; *New Mexico Business Directory For 1909–1910* (Denver: The Gazetteer Publishing Co., 1909), 877–80; *New Mexico Business Directory For 1913–1914* (Denver: The Gazetteer Publishing Co., 1914), 845–49; *New Mexico State Business Directory 1920* (Denver: The Gazetteer Publishing Co., 1920), 601; *New Mexico State Business Directory 1922* (Denver: The Gazetteer Publishing Co., 1922), 580; *New Mexico State Business Directory 1930* (Denver: The Gazetteer Publishing Co., 1930), 686; *New Mexico State Business Directory 1940–41* (Denver: The Gazetteer Publishing Co., 1940), 734–35; *New Mexico State Business Directory 1950* (Albuquerque: University of New Mexico Printing Plant, 1950), 138–39; *Southern Pacific Coast Directory; for 1888–9* (San Francisco: McKenney Directory Company, publisher, April 1888), 438–48.

*Advertisements in *Santa Fe, New Mexico: The Ancient City*
(Santa Fe: Santa Fe Chamber of Commerce, 1929).

The directories were found at the Museum of New Mexico unless noted otherwise.

TOURISM STATISTICS (LODGERS' TAX REPORTS)

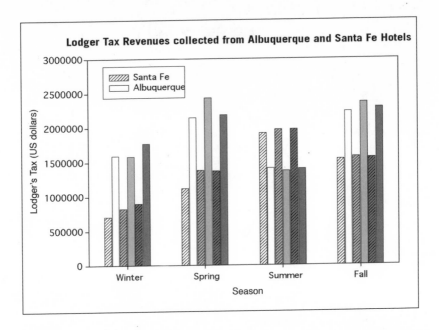

Lodger Tax Revenues collected from Albuquerque and Santa Fe Hotels

Vertical bars reflect data for 1999 (white), 2000 (gray), and 2001 (dark gray).

Years are not significantly different (df = 2. MS = $1.1*10^{10}$, F = 2.66, P > 0.14)

When the cities are compared across seasons, however, it is clear that Santa Fe has higher revenues than Albuquerque in summer (tourist season), but lower in all other seasons. This is borne out in a statistically significant interaction between season and city (df = 3, MS = $7.6*10^{11}$, F = 184, P < 0.0001).

Seasons differ from each other significant. (df = 3, MS = $5.4*10^{11}$, F = 129.89, P < 0.0001) Using a Scheffe a posteriori test, autumn fees are significantly higher than summer and spring (corresponding with the Albuquerque International Balloon Fiesta), which in turn are significantly higher than winter.

Cities differ from each other (df = 1, MS = $1.5*10^{12}$, F = 357.40, P < 0.0001), with Albuquerque raising more lodgers' fees than Santa Fe.

Analysis: three-way analysis of variance with fixed effects, analyzing the influence of year, season, and city (plus all two-way interactions) on lodgers' taxes.

Notes

Introduction

1.   The Atchison Topeka and Santa Fe Railroad will be referred to as the AT&SF, the Santa Fe Railroad, or the Atchison, Topeka, and Santa Fe Railroad.

2.   Leah Dilworth, *Imagining Indians in the Southwest: Persistent Visions of a Primitive Past* (Washington, D.C.: Smithsonian Press, 1996), 17.

3.   Ibid.

4.   Ibid., Diane H. Thomas, *The Southwestern Indian Detours* (Phoenix: Hunter Publishing Co., 1978).

5.   Chris Wilson, *The Myth of Santa Fe: Creating a Modern Regional Tradition* (Albuquerque: University of New Mexico Press, 1997); Peter Hertzog, *La Fonda: The Inn of Santa Fe* (Portales: Bishop Printing and Litho. Co., 1962).

6.   For the history of the Santa Fe Railroad, see Merle Armitage, *Operations Santa Fe* (New York: Duell, Sloan and Pearce, 1948); Glen D. Bradley, *The Story of the Santa Fe* (Boston: The Gorham Press, 1920); Keith L. Bryant, Jr., *History of the Atchison, Topeka, and Santa Fe Railway* (New York: Macmillan Publishing Co., 1974); Donald Duke, *Santa Fe: The Railroad Gateway to the American West*. Volume 2 (San Marino: Golden Books, 1995); James Marshall, *Santa Fe, the Railroad that Built the Empire* (New York: Random House, 1945); and John Moody, *The Railroad Builders* (New Haven: Yale University Press, 1919). For the history of the Fred Harvey Company and the Harvey Girls, see Samuel Hopkins Adams, *The Harvey Girls* (Cleveland: World Publishing Company, 1942); Donald Duke, *Fred Harvey, Civilizer of the American Southwest* (Arcada: Pregel Press, 1995); James Davis Henderson, *Meals by Fred Harvey; A Phenomenon of the American West* (Fort Worth: Texas Christian University Press, 1969); Kathleen L. Howard and Diana F. Pardue, *Inventing the Southwest: The Fred Harvey Company and Native American Art* (Flagstaff: Northland Publishing Company, 1996); Lesley Poling-Kempes, *Far From Home: West by Rail with the Harvey Girls* (Lubbock: Texas Tech University Press, 1994); and *The Harvey Girls: Women Who Opened the West* (New York: Paragon House, 1989); Juddi Morris, *The Harvey Girls: The Women Who Civilized the West* (New York: Walker and Co., 1994); and Marta Weigle and Barbara A. Babcock, eds., *The Great Southwest of the Fred Harvey Company and the Santa Fe Railway* (Phoenix: The Heard Museum, 1996). For the history of Santa Fe, New Mexico, see Paul Horgan, *The Centuries of Santa Fe* (New York: E. P. Dutton and Co., 1965); David Grant Noble, ed., *Santa Fe: History of an Ancient City* (Santa Fe: School of American Research Press, 1989); Marc Simmons, *Yesterday in Santa Fe* (Cerrillos, NM: San Marcos Press, 1969); and Henry J. Tobias and Charles E. Woodhouse, *Santa Fe: A Modern History, 1880–1990* (Albuquerque: University of New Mexico Press, 2001).

7.   Greever discussed how the AT&SF secured and exchanged land in efforts to obtain property in essential locations throughout the Southwest. William S. Greever, *Arid Domain: The Santa Fe Railway and Its Western Land Grant* (Stanford: Stanford University Press, 1954).

Chapter One

1. Patricia Nelson Limerick, "Seeing and Being Seen: Tourism in the American West," in *Over the Edge: Remapping of the American West*, ed. Valerie J. Matsumoto and Blake Allmendinger (Berkeley: University of California Press, 1999), 29.

2. Joe S. Sando, *Pueblo Nations: Eight Centuries of Pueblo History* (Santa Fe: Clear Light Publishers, 1992), 44.

3. Gabrielle G. Palmer, *El Camino Real de Tierra Adentro* (Santa Fe: New Mexico Bureau of Land Management, No. 11, 1963), 16.

4. Max L. Moorhead, *New Mexico's Royal Road: Trade and Travel on the Chihuahua Trail* (Norman: University of Oklahoma Press. 1958), 7.

5. Douglas Preston, "The Granddaddy of the Nation's Trail Began in Mexico." *Smithsonian* 26, No. 8 (November 1995), 142.

6. Sando, *Pueblo Nations,* 62.

7. Marc Simmons, *The Last Conquistador: Juan de Oñate and the Settlement of the Far Southwest* (Norman: University of Oklahoma Press, 1991), 131–55.

8. Bertha P. Dutton, *Indians of the Southwest* (Englewood Cliffs, NJ: Prentice-Hall, 1975), 20; Sando, *Pueblo Nations,* 7.

9. Ramón A. Gutiérrez, *When Jesus Came, the Corn Mothers Went Away* (Stanford: Stanford University Press, 1991), 306–8; Sando, *Pueblo Nations,* 45.

10. Charles F. Lummis, "Santa Fe: The Capital of Our Romance," *Old Santa Fe and Roundabout* (Chicago: Hedstrom-Barry Co., Printers, 1923), 6, California State Railroad Museum (hereafter cited as CSRRM).

11. Joe S. Sando, *Pueblo Profiles* (Santa Fe: Clear Light Publishing, 1998), 8–10.

12. L. L. Waters, *Steel Trails of Santa Fe* (Lawrence: University of Kansas Press, 1950), 14–15; Andrew L. Knaut. *The Pueblo Revolt of 1680: Conquest and Resistance in Seventeenth-Century New Mexico* (Norman: University of Oklahoma, 1995).

13. Knaut, *Pueblo Revolt*; Horgan, *Centuries of Santa Fe,* 42–90; Sando, *Pueblo Nations,* 63–68.

14. Moorhead, *New Mexico's Royal Road,* 49–54.

15. Ibid.; *Santa Fe Fiesta, Official Program* (Santa Fe: Santa Fe New Mexican Publishing Corporation, 1929), 20, Museum of New Mexico (hereafter cited as MNM).

16. From the beginning of Mexico's National Period in 1821, trade barriers with the United Sates were eliminated. In 1822, William Becknell of Missouri inaugurated commercial relations between Missouri and New Mexico via what became known as the Santa Fe Trail. For more information on the Santa Fe Trail, see Larry Beachum, *William Becknell: Father of the Santa Fe Trade* (El Paso: Texas Western Press, 1982); Peter Gerhard, *The Northern Frontier of New Spain* (Norman: University of Oklahoma Press, 1993); Moorhead, *New Mexico's Royal Road*; Palmer, *El Camino Real de Tierra Adentro*; Preston, "Granddaddy of the Nation's Trails."

17. Janet Lecompte, *Rebellion in Rio Arriba 1837* (Albuquerque: University of New Mexico Press, 1985), 7–11.

18. Ibid., 13.

19. Ibid., 20.

20. Ibid., 43.

21. Calvin Horn. *New Mexico's Troubled Years* (Albuquerque: Horn and Wallace Publishers, 1963), 21–22, 96; Sando. *Pueblo Nations*, 86.

22. Erna Fergusson, *New Mexico: A Pageant of Three Peoples* (New York: Alfred A. Knopf, 1951), 257–59.

23. Paul Horgan, *Great River: The Rio Grande in North American History*, 2: 765–68.

24. Susan A. Roberts and Calvin A. Roberts, *New Mexico* (Albuquerque: University of New Mexico Press, 1988), 108.

25. Thomas C. Donnelly, *The Government of New Mexico* (Albuquerque: The University of New Mexico Press, 1947), 57; Horgan, *Great River*, 2:779–801; Michael C. Meyer and William L. Sherman, *The Course of Mexican History*, 5th ed., (New York: Oxford University Press, 1995), 351–53; David J. Weber, *New Spain's Far Northern Frontier* (Dallas: Southern Methodist University Press, 1979), 5, 9, 12.

26. Roberts and Roberts, *New Mexico*, 124; Marc Simmons, *New Mexico: A Bicentennial History* (New York: W. W. Norton and Company, 1977), 147.

27. Marc Simmons, "Santa Fe in the Days of the Trail," in *Santa Fe: History of an Ancient City*, ed. David Grant Noble (Santa Fe: School of American Research Press, 1989), 127.

28. Bryant, *History*, 164; Horgan says seventeen miles in *Centuries of Santa Fe*, 272.

29. "Santa Fe's Triumph," *Weekly New Mexican*, February 14, 1880.

30. Bradley, *History of the Atchison, Topeka, and Santa Fe Railway*, 84–86.

31. Ibid., 147; Waters, *Steel Rails of Santa Fe*, 54–55.

32. Bradley, *Story of Santa Fe*, 149; Marshall, *Santa Fe*, 131.

33. Moody, *Railroad Builders*, 158.

34. Marshall, *Santa Fe*, 131.

35. Bradley, *Story of Santa Fe*, 150–61; Bryant, *History*, 43–46; Marshall, *Santa Fe*, 129–31.

36. Marshall, *Santa Fe*, 130–32.

37. Bradley, *Story of Santa Fe*, 206; Bryant, *History*, 62.

38. Lucius Beebe and Charles Clegg, *Rio Grande: Mainline of the Rockies* (Berkeley: Howell-North Books, 1962), 12.

39. Bradley, *Story of Santa Fe*, 204.

40. Bryant, *History*, 60–62.

41. *Weekly New Mexican*, July 19, 1879, 2.

42. *Weekly New Mexican*, February 14, 1880, 2.

43. *Santa Fe* (New York: Sanborn Map Company, 1880), California State Library, (hereafter cited as CSL), Mirofilm 42, Reel 3; *Compendium of the Tenth Census of the U.S.* (Washington, D.C.: U.S. Government Printing Office, 1885), 394.

44. Santa Fe Chamber of Commerce, telephone inquiry, September 26, 2000; *1998/1999 Santa Fe NM Polk City Directory*, 1998, 48.

45. *Indian-detour* (Topeka: Atchison, Topeka and Santa Fe Railway Co., 1926), 6, MNM.

46. *Old-New Santa Fe and Roundabout* (Topeka: The Atchison, Topeka and Santa Fe Railway Co., 1916), 6, CSRRM.

47. *Resources of New Mexico* (Santa Fe: New Mexico Book and Job Printing Department, 1881), 4, New Mexico State Records and Archives (hereafter cited

as NMSRA).

48. Miguel A. Otero, *Report of the Governor of New Mexico to the Secretary of the Interior, 1903* (Washington, D.C.: Government Printing Office, 1903), 360.

49. T. C. McLuhan, *Dream Tracks: The Railroad and the American Indian, 1890–1930* (New York: Harry N. Abrams, 1985), 13–29.

Chapter Two

1. Earl Pomeroy, *In Search of the Golden West: The Tourist in Western America* (New York: Alfred A. Knopf, 1957), 19.

2. McLuhan, *Dream Tracks,* 13–29.

3. Pomeroy, *In Search of the Old West,* vii.

4. Ibid., 8.

5. Philip J. Deloria, *Playing Indian* (New Haven: Yale University Press, 1998), 3.

6. John E. Baur, *The Health Seekers of Southern California, 1870–1900* (San Marino: The Huntington Library, 1959), 6–22.

7. Ibid., 29.

8. Billy M. Jones, *Health-Seekers in the Southwest, 1817–1900* (Norman: University of Oklahoma Press, 1967), 29–30.

9. Jake W. Spidel, Jr., *Doctors of Medicine in New Mexico* (Albuquerque: The University of New Mexico Press, 1986), 97.

10. *The New Southwest: New Mexico Rio Grande Valley, Arizona Salt River Valley* (Chicago: Rand, McNally & Co., circa 1895), Kansas State Historical Society (hereafter cited as KSHS), 15, GL 917.89 pam. v. 2, 35245. The brochure states that "a sanatorium and a hospital, occupy prominent locations in the city."

11. Ibid.

12. Ibid., 15; Tobias and Woodhouse, *Santa Fe,* 60.

13. Rev. Edward Willcocks Meany, *Santa Fe as a Health Resort* (Santa Fe: New Mexican Printing Co., 1890), available in MNM, file 108.

14. Bushrod W. James, A. M., M.D., *American Resorts With Notes Upon Their Climate* (Philadelphia: F. A. Davis, 1889), 9–11, 158–59; Jones, *Health-Seekers in the Southwest,* 166–69.

15. Meany, *Santa Fe as a Health Resort,* 1.

16. William G. Ritch, *Illustrated New Mexico* (Santa Fe: New Mexican Printing and Publishing, 1883), NMSRA.

17. These publications include *A Colorado Summer, Las Vegas Hot Springs and Vicinity, Health Resorts in Salt River Valley, Arizona, Grand Canyon of the Colorado River in Arizona*, and *To California and Back*, as noted in *Resorts on the Santa Fe* (N.p.: Santa Fe Passenger Department, 1898), 3, KSHS.

18. *New Mexico Health Resorts* (Topeka: Passenger Department of the AT & SF RW, 1897), 46, KSHS, GL 917.89 pam. v. 2.

19. Ibid., 49.

20. Ibid.

21. "Reasons Why the Santa Fe is the most Comfortable Summer Route to California." *Santa Fe All the Way* (Chicago: The Henry O. Shepard Co., 1907), 3, KSHS, K 385 AT 2 pam. v. 8.

22. James, *American Resorts,* 97–98.

23. Steven D. Fox, "Healing, Imagination, and New Mexico," *New Mexico*

Historical Review 58 (July 1983), 218.

24. *New Mexico Health Resorts,* 45–49.

25. Ibid., 46.

26. Phone interview with Mary Thomas, Concierge at the Bishop's Lodge, April 24, 2001.

27. "The Bishop's Lodge in Old Santa Fe," *The Santa Fe Magazine* (September 1924), 57, All articles in *The Santa Fe Magazine* were collected at the KSHS, file No. 385 At 2, unless cited otherwise. *The Santa Fe Magazine* was published primarily for the employees of the railroad. The first printing was in 1906 and continued until 1983.

28. Ibid.

29. Ibid., 57.

30. Ibid., 58.

31. "The Oldest Health Resort in America," *The Santa Fe Magazine* (September 1933), 20, KSHS, 385 At 2.

32. Ibid., 21; Jones, *Health-Seekers in the Southwest,* 166.

33. Fox, "Healing, Imagination, and New Mexico," 214.

34. Spidel, *Doctors of Medicine,* 163.

35. Ceo. T. Nicholson, *New Mexico* (Topeka: Gen. Passenger and Ticket Agent A.T. & S.F. R.R., n.d.), flyer, MNM, vertical files, AC024-P.

36. *New Mexico: A Land of Prosperity and Happiness* (Chicago: Rand, McNally & Co., 1891), 2–3, KSHS, 385-At 2, pam v. 8.

37. *Agriculture and Horticulture* (Santa Fe; New Mexico Printing Co., 1898), 38–45, KSHS, GL 917.89, pam v. 2.

38. *Ho! To the Land of Sunshine: A Guide to New Mexico for the Homeseeker* (Albuquerque: New Mexico Bureau of Immigration, 1909), 3–19, KSHS, GL 917.89, pam. v. 2.

39. Ibid., 39.

40. Ibid.

41. Ibid.

42. *New Mexico* (Chicago: Poole Bros., 1910), 34, KSHS, GL 385 At 2, pam. v. 8.

43. Ibid., 34.

44. Ibid., 48.

45. *Ninth Census of the United States* (Washington, D.C.: U.S. Government Printing Office, 1871), v. 1, 206, *Fourteenth Census of the United States* (Washington, D.C.: U.S. Government Printing Office, 1921), v. 1, 529.

46. *Fourteenth Census of the United States* (Washington, D.C.: U.S. Government Printing Office, 1921), v. 4, 119.

47. Tucson was used because of its comparable population census in the late 1800s to Santa Fe and the fact that it is on the Southern Pacific Company's line. *Fifteenth Census of the United States* (Washington, D.C.: U.S. Government Printing Office, 1921), v. 1, 92.

48. Ibid., 1097. Provo was used for a contrast in population census because of its isolation from the transcontinental rail lines.

49. Bradley, *Story of Santa Fe,* 294, 300, 302. The Atchison Topeka and Santa Fe Railway Company Records at the Kansas State Historical do not have any records regarding the number of tickets sold to passengers going to Santa Fe,

New Mexico, or the cost of each ticket. In "Winter Excursion Fares to Summerland," *daily Xcursions* (Chicago: Rand McNally & Company, 1925) 111–12, University of New Mexico Center for Southwest Research (hereafter cited as CSWR); round-trip ticket to Santa Fe from Chicago in 1925 cost $78.85.

50. Wilson, *Myth of Santa Fe,* 89; Sandra D'Emelio and Susan Campbell, *Visions and Visionaries: The Art and Artists of the Santa Fe Railway* (Salt Lake City: Peregrine Smith Books, 1991), 131–33.

51. Dilworth, *Imagining Indians,* 17; McLuhan, *Dream Tracks,* 31.

52. Duke, *Santa Fe,* 2:529. See Jane Eliot, *The History of the Western Railroads* (New York: Exeter Books, 1985), 145, for examples of the Santa Fe logo.

53. Deloria, *Playing Indian,* 183, 191.

54. McLuhan, *Dream Tracks,* 13, 15.

55. Ibid., 20.

56. Ibid.; Wilson, *Myth of Santa Fe,* 90.

57. Duke, *Fred Harvey,* 532. For more information about the Santa Fe logos, emblems, and promotional materials that were borrowed from Navajo blankets, pottery, and baskets, see Armitage, *Operations of the Santa Fe,* 111–25; and McLuhan, *Dream Tracks,* 19–20.

58. Wilson, *Myth of Santa Fe,* 93; Hal K. Rothman, *Devil's Bargains: Tourism in the Twentieth-Century American West* (Lawrence: University Press of Kansas, 1998), 54–55. Elsewhere, the railroad began to promote tourism. The main tourist attraction for the Santa Fe started in 1901 and was the Grand Canyon. One could take the spur from Williams, Arizona, to the Grand Canyon for $3.95. By 1905, the Fred Harvey Company's famous El Tovar opened its doors for tourists.

59. Ibid.

60. Wilson, *Myth of Santa Fe,* 331; *Business Directory of New Mexico and Gazetteer of the Territory* (Santa Fe: New Mexico Printing & Publishing Co., 1882), CSL microfilm 549, reel 120. Hotel counts and lodging rooms were based on the above sources and the plans of insurance maps of the Sanborn Map Company, 1882; 1886; 1890; 1898; 1902; 1908; 1913; 1913; 1921; 1930, CSL microfilm 242, reel 3.

61. Dilworth, *Imagining Indians,* 17; Wilson, *Myth of Santa Fe,* 93–94; See Appendix A for a list of publications that the AT&SF used to promote Santa Fe.

62. See Appendix A.

63. Adolph F. Bandelier, *The Delight Makers* (New York: Dodd, Mead and Co., 1890), preface.

64. Mary Austin, *The Land of Little Rain* (Boston: Houghton Mifflin and Co., 1903); Charles Lummis, *A New Mexico David and Other Stories and Sketches of the Southwest* (New York: Scribner and Sons, 1905).

65. Quoted in Lawrence Clark Powell, *Southwest Classics* (Los Angeles: Ward Ritchie Press, 1974), 99.

66. Quoted in ibid., 99–100.

67. Charles Lummis, *Letters from the Southwest,* ed. James W. Byrkit (Tucson: The University of Arizona Press, 1989), xi. Some studies of Lummis are Edwin F. Bingham, *Charles F. Lummis, Editor of the Southwest* (San Marino: Huntington Library, 1955); Dudley Gordon, *Charles F. Lummis, Crusader in Corduroy* (Los Angeles: Cultural Assets Press, 1972); Daniela P. Moneta, ed. *Chas. F. Lummis – The Centennial Exhibition* (Los Angeles: Southwest Museum, 1985); Powell,

Southwest Classics; W. W. Robinson, *The Story of the Southwest Museum* (Los Angeles: Ward Ritchie Press, 1960).

68. Pomeroy, *In Search of the Golden West*, 37.

69. The writers under contract with the Santa Fe included George A. Dorsey, Zane Grey, Charles Lummis, and Ralph Twitchell.

70. Ralph E. Twitchell, "An Old-world City in the New; The Place that Gave Santa Fe its Name," *Old-New Santa Fe and Roundabout* (n.p.: The Atchison, Topeka and Santa Fe Railway Co., 1912), 2, MNM. The AT&SF had several publishers that produced advertising materials. They include, but were not limited to, the Passenger Department of the AT&SF, Rand McNally, Henry O. Shepard Co., *The Santa Fe Magazine, National Geographic, Land of Sunshine*, New Mexico Bureau of Immigration, Poole Brothers, New Mexico Printing Co., Fred Harvey, Hedstrom-Barry Co. Printers, Newman-Monroe, and the *Santa Fe New Mexican*.

71. Rita C. Velásquez, ed., *Directory of American Scholars*, v. 1, 9th ed. (Detroit: The Gale Group, 1998), 1135.

72. Ibid.

73. Powell, *Southwest Classics,* 13–15, 307, 43–51; Twitchell, "An Old-world City in the New; The Place that Gave Santa Fe its Name," *Old-New Santa Fe and Roundabout* (1912), 2. Twitchell's suggestions included Josiah Gregg's *Commerce of the Prairies*, a descriptive narrative of Gregg's life as a Santa Fe trader, who initially came to Santa Fe for its pleasant climate and for health reasons; Theodore Roosevelt's *Winning of the West*, which owed much to Lummis. The president's former college classmate, Lummis advised Roosevelt on irrigation, Indian welfare, and archeological sites. Twitchell also recommended Lummis's *The Flute of the Gods* and *The Land Of Enchantment*, both about New Mexico and its people.

74. Zane Grey, "An Appreciation of New Mexico," *Santa Fe: The Gateway of the "Greatest Fifty Mile Square in America," The Santa Fe New Mexican* (circa 1918), 2, MNM.

75. Ibid., 2.

76. Lawrence Clark Powell's foreword in Mary A. Sarber, *Charles F. Lummis: A Bibliography* (Tucson: University of Arizona, 1977), vii.

77. Charles F. Lummis, "Santa Fe: The Capital of Our Romance," *Old Santa Fe and Roundabout* (1912), 5, MNM.

78. Ibid., 5.

79. Ibid., 10.

80. *Old-New Santa Fe and the Roundabout* (1912), 2, 6.

81. "Indian Ceremonies," *Roads to Yesterday: Motor Drives Out from Old Santa Fé* (Chicago: Hestorm-Barry Co., 1927), 18, MNM.

82. Ross Calvin, *Sky Determines* (MacMillan Company, 1934; repr., Silver City: High-Lonesome Books, 1993), 212.

83. Charles Lummis, ed., *Land Of Sunshine: The Magazine for California and the West* (Los Angeles: Land of Sunshine Publishing Company, 1895).

84. Edward Hungerford, "A Study in Consistent Railroad Advertising," *The Santa Fe Magazine* (March 1923), 43, KSHS, 385 At2.

85. Ibid.

86. Ibid., 48.

87. Ibid., 46. Some of the publications used by the AT&SF to promote Santa Fe

before 1925 include *The Earth*, July 1907; *Land of Sunshine*, November 1898; *National Geographic*, May 1924; *Publisher's Weekly*, March 1925.

88.   Poling-Kempes, *Harvey Girls*, 35–36; Waters, *Steel Trails of Santa Fe*, 276.

Chapter Three

1.   Henderson, *Meals by Fred Harvey*, 2.
2.   Marshall, *Santa Fe*, 97.
3.   Henderson, *Meals by Fred Harvey*, 3.
4.   Marshall, *Santa Fe*, 98.
5.   Ibid.
6.   Morris, *Harvey Girls*, 10–11.
7.   Henderson, *Meals by Fred Harvey*, 35–36.
8.   For more information regarding the Harvey Girls, see Adams, *Harvey Girls*; Poling-Kempes, *Far From Home*, and *Harvey Girls*; Morris, *Harvey Girls*; and Weigle and Babcock, *Great Southwest*.
9.   Henderson, *Meals by Fred Harvey*, 20; Marshall, *Santa Fe*, 100.
10.   Henderson, *Meals by Fred Harvey*, 21; Marshall, *Santa Fe*, 101.
11.   Morris, *Harvey Girls*, 37.
12.   Henderson, *Meals by Fred Harvey*, 20–21.
13.   Dilworth, *Imagining Indians*, 80–92; Thomas, *Southwestern Indian Detours*, 10–37.
14.   David F. Myrick, *New Mexico's Railroads*, rev. ed. (Albuquerque: University of New Mexico Press, 1990), 34.
15.   *Santa Fe Republican*, June 8, 1848, MNM, Vertical Files, "Hotels."
16.   "Passing of a Landmark," *The Santa Fe Magazine* (July 1913), 54.
17.   *Daily New Mexican*, March 6, 1881, p. 4, c.1; Hertzog, *La Fonda*, 21.
18.   *"La Fonda" At the End of the Santa Fe Trail.* Brochure (Publisher not known, circa 1921), MNM; "Santa Fe's New Hotel," *The Santa Fe Magazine* (December 1920), 26. MNM, Vertical Files, "Hotels;" Virginia L. Grattan, *Mary Colter: Builder Upon Red Earth* (Flagstaff: Northland Press, 1980), 50.
19.   Hertzog, *La Fonda*, 25.
20.   Carl D. Sheppard, *Creator of the Santa Fe Style: Isaac Hamilton Rapp, Architect* (Albuquerque: University of New Mexico Press, 1988), 94–95.
21.   "Santa Fe's New Hotel," *The Santa Fe Magazine* (December 1920), 26, KSHS.
22.   Julian Cavalier, *Classic American Railroad Stations* (San Diego: A. S. Barnes and Co., 1980), 150; Charles C. Eldredge, Julie Schimmel, and William H., Truettner, *Art in Mew Mexico 1900–1945: Paths to Taos and Santa Fe* (New York: Abbeville Press, 1986), 105; Christine Mather, ed., *Colonial Frontiers: Art and Life in Spanish New Mexico, The Fred Harvey Collection* (Santa Fe: Ancient City Press, 1983), 95.
23.   May Colter was responsible for the architectural designs of the El Navajo (opened in 1923) and La Posada (opened in 1930). She fashioned these two properties after Rapp's La Fonda. Weigle and Babcock, *Great Southwest*, xv–xvi.
24.   "Sub-Committee Plan Fails to Furnish Quick action Upon La Fonda," *Santa Fe New Mexican*, February 5, 1922, p. 2, col. 3, 4, 5; "Fonda Hotel Case Set for March Eight," *Santa Fe New Mexican*, March 3, 1922, p. 3, col. 3.
25.   "Fred Harvey Takes over La Fonda: Big Crew Installed to Operate Santa Fe

Hotel," *Santa Fe New Mexican*, May 1, 1926, p. 5, col. 1 and 2; Letter to Earl D. Richie, from N. J. Barker, with Laughlin and Barker, Attorneys at law, November 16, 1921, NMSR, N. B. Laughlin Papers No. 12.

26. Marta Weigle, "Exposition and Mediation: Mary Colter, Erna Fergusson, and the Santa Fe/Fred Harvey Popularization of the Native Southwest, 1902–1940," *Frontiers*12, No. 3 (Niwot: University Press of Colorado, 1992), 128–29.

27. Grattan, *Mary Colter*, 4.

28. Ibid.

29. Erna Fergusson, *Our Southwest* (New York: Knopf, 1940), 203–4.

30. "Indian-detours Charm Eastern Writer," *The Santa Fe Magazine* (January 1929), 31–32.

31. The author has visited the hotel annually for the last decade, and although it was enlarged again in 1950, it remains much the way it was photographed in the 1930s. The "Santa Fe Style," created by Mary E. Colter, is documented in Grattan, *Mary Colter*, 50–57; Sandra D. Lynn, *Windows of the Past: Historical Lodging of New Mexico* (Albuquerque: University of New Mexico Press, 1999), 36, 40–44; Marshall, *Santa Fe*; Waters, *Steel Trails of Santa Fe*, 279; and Duke, *Santa Fe*, 2:380; Wilson, *Myth of Santa Fe*, 139.

32. Duke, *Fred Harvey*, 380.

33. Thomas, *Southwestern Indian Detours*, 201–3.

34. Artwork is featured in *Harvey Motor Cruises Off the Beaten Path in the Great Southwest* (Chicago: Rand McNally & Co., 1928), 15–16, MNM; *La Fonda: The Inn at the End of the Trail in Old Santa Fe, New Mexico* (Chicago: Rand McNally, 1929), 5, MNM, Vertical Files, "Hotels."

35. *La Fonda: The Inn at the End of the Trail in Old Santa Fe, New Mexico*, 5; Thomas, *Southwestern Indian Detours*, 202.

36. Duke, *Fred Harvey*, 380.

37. Weigle, "Exposition and Mediation," 119–20.

38. Quote by D'Emilio in John Villani's article, "Artists Took Ride on the Santa Fe," *New Mexico Magazine* 69, No. 11 (November 1991), 53.

39. Armitage, *Operation Santa Fe*, 118; Eldredge, Schimmel, and Truettner, *Art in New Mexico*, 13–14, 81.

40. Arrell Morgan Gibson, *The Santa Fe and Taos Colonies: Age of the Muses, 1900–1942* (Norman: University of Oklahoma Press, 1983), 57; Weigle, "Exposition and Mediation," 119.

41. Eldredge, Schimmel, and Truettner, *Art in New Mexico*, 13; John A. Berger, *Fernand Lungren* (Santa Barbara: Schauer Press, 1936), 55–59.

42. Eldredge, Schimmel, and Truettner, *Art in New Mexico*, 204.

43. Fred Harvey Collection, Heard Museum (hereafter cited as HM). See Appendix D.

44. Eldredge, Schimmel, and Truettner, *Art in New Mexico*, 14.

45. Ibid., 194.

46. McLuhan, *Dream Tracks*, 29; Weigle and Babcock, *Great Southwest*, 150.

47. Eldredge, Schimmel, and Truettner, *Art in New Mexico*, 182.

48. See *Harveycar Motor Cruises off the beaten path in the Great Southwest* (October 1928), 43–46.

49. Howard and Pardue, *Inventing the Southwest*, 96–98.

50.   Bryant, *History,* 437–53, George A. Dorsey, *Indians of the Southwest* (Chicago: Passenger Department of the AT & SFRW, 1903), HMA; Van Deren Coke, *Taos and Santa Fe: The Artists' Environment* (Albuquerque: University of New Mexico Press, 1963); Gibson, *Santa Fe and Taos Colonies.*

51.   Gibson, *Santa Fe and Taos Colonies,* 34.

52.   Weigle, "Exposition and Meditation," 137.

53.   Examples of Lungren's work were featured in *Harper's Weekly, Century Magazine,* and *St. Nicholas Magazine.* Sharp's work graced the pages of *McClure's Magazine;* see Keith L. Bryant, "The Atchison, Topeka and Santa Fe Railway and the Development of the Taos and Santa Fe Art Colonies," *Western Historical Quarterly* 9 (1979), 439, KSHS.

54.   Paul A. Walter, "The Santa Fe-Taos Art Movement," *Art and Archeology* 4 (December 1916), 330–38.

55.   Bryant, "Atchison, Topeka and Santa Fe Railway," 446–53; Gibson, *Santa Fe and Taos Colonies,* 34, 250. Tourists began to travel once again after World War I.

56.   Dilworth, *Imagining Indians,* 91.

57.   Thomas, *Southwestern Indian Detours,* 37.

58.   *New Mexico Business Directory 1920* (Denver: The Gazetteer Publishing Co., 1920), 605; Wilson, *Myth of Santa Fe,* 331.

59.   "Winter Excursion Fares to Summerland," *The Atchison, Topeka & Santa Fe Railway System Time Table* (Chicago: Rand McNally & Company, February, 1925) 11112, CSWR, Collection MSS 115 (BC), Box 1, Folder 13.

60.   Rodger William Birdseye, "The Indian Detour," *The Santa Fe Magazine* (April 1926), 45. KSHS; "Santa Fe Will Establish Bus Detour Through Indian Pueblos," *Albuquerque Morning Journal,* August 20, 1925, p. 1, col. 8, p. 2, col. 2.

61.   Dilworth, *Imagining Indians,* 91; Thomas, *Southwestern Indian Detours,* 39–40.

62.   Thomas, *Southwestern Indian Detours,* 44.

63.   Ibid., 43–44; "Santa Fe Will Establish Bus Detour Through Indian Pueblos," *Albuquerque Morning Journal,* August 20, 1925, p. 1, col. 8, p. 2, col. 2.

64.   Rothman, *Devil's Bargains,* 158.

65.   Ibid.

66.   Thomas, *Southwestern Indian Detours,* 43–44; "Santa Fe Will Establish Bus Detour Through Indian Pueblos," *Albuquerque Morning Journal,* August 20, 1925, p. 1, col. 8, p. 2, col. 2.

67.   "Fifty Thousand Tourists Will Traverse State," *Albuquerque Morning Journal,* August 21, 1925, p. 1., col. 7.

68.   *The Indian-detour* (Chicago: Rand McNally and Co., 1925). This publication became an annual brochure containing updated information on excursion prices and a variety of tours for tourists to choose from. Additionally, passengers on board the Santa Fe received a copy of *Old-New Santa Fe and Roundabout,* which contained maps and photos of places to go and see in Santa Fe. This brochure sought to persuade travelers to stop and see these sites. *Old-New Santa Fe and Roundabout* (Chicago: Press of the Henry O. Shepard Co., May 1916), CSRRM; Thomas, *Southwestern Indian Detours,* 58.

69.   "Traffic Head For Santa Fe Seeing Detour," *Albuquerque Morning Journal,* August 31, 1925, p. 1, col. 7.

70.   *Indian Detours-Most Distinctive Motor Cruise Service in the World* (Chicago:

Rand McNally, 1930), 1–8, NMSRA, No. 6491.

71. *Harvey Motor Cruises Off the Beaten Path in the Great Southwest* (1928), 81, MNM; "Harveycar Motor Cruises," *Santa Fe Magazine* (July 1929), 23, KSHS.

72. Dilworth, *Imagining Indians,* 92. A collection of these promotional items is available in the archives at the Heard Museum in Phoenix, Arizona.

73. Thomas, *Southwestern Indian Detours,* 77.

74. *Indian-detour* (1926), 3–4. MNM.

75. Ibid., 6.

76. "First of Santa Fe Indian Detour Trips is Completed, Tourists From All Parts of the World Like It, Journal Writer Tells Impression of Bus Journey," *Albuquerque Morning Journal,* May 18, 1926, p.1, col. 3,5, NMSRA.

77. "What Tourists Think of Detour," *Albuquerque Morning Journal,* May 18, 1926, p.1, col. 6, CSWR.

78. "Woman Leads Tourists," *The Philadelphia Inquirer,* March 15, 1926, CSWR, MMS 45, Scrapbook No. 1, Box 1922–27; Thomas, *Southwestern Indian Detours,* 75.

79. "Women Guides, de Lux," *The Philadelphia Inquirer,* March 25, 1927, CSWR, Collection No. MMS 45 Scrapbook No. 1, Box 1922–27; Weigle and Babcock, *Great Southwest,* 50.

80. Marta Weigle and Peter White, *The Lore of New Mexico* (Albuquerque: University of New Mexico Press, 1988), 59; "The Motor Cruise Courier of the Great Southwest," *Pacific Coast Hotel Weekly* (March 15, 1930), NMSA, R. Hunter Clarkson Collection No. 8251; "Director of Unique Courier Service Tells How Plan Was Developed," *Pittsburgh Press,* May 21, 1930, NMSA, Clarkson Collection; Thomas, *Southwestern Indian Detours,* 76–94.

81. Thomas, *Southwestern Indian Detours,* 88.

82. "Women Guides, de Lux," *The Philadelphia Inquirer,* CSWR, MMS 45, Scrapbook No. 1, Box 1922–27.

83. Poem for Miss Fergusson. CSWR, Collection No. MMS 45 Scrapbook No. 1, Box 1922–27.

84. "Miss Fergusson Resigns From Indian Detours," *Santa Fe New Mexican* (September 23, 1927), NMSA, No. MMS 45 Scrapbook No. 2; "'Dude Wrangler' Miss Fergusson No Longer With the Indian Detour," *The Santa Fe New Mexican* (n.d.), CSWR, Collection No. MMS 45, Scrapbook No. 1, Box 1922–27.

85. "The Courier Corps, a Unique Service Feature," *Harveycars Motor Cruises: Off the Beaten Path in the Great Southwest* (Topeka: Atchison Topeka & Santa Fe Railway Company, 1928), 11–12.

86. Dilworth, *Imagining Indians,* 92; Thomas, *Southwestern Indian Detours,* 82.

87. "Miss Henrietta Gloff, One of the Couriers to The Last Frontier," *Observer* (March 15, 1930), NMSRA, Clarkson Collection; Weigle and Babcock, *Great Southwest,* 54.

88. Thomas, *Southwestern Indian Detours,* 91.

89. Letter to H. R. Clarkson from Benj. F. Shambaugh, (April 8, 1928), NMSA, Konopek File No. 6491.

90. Quoted in Thomas, *Southwestern Indian Detours,* 84.

91. Ibid., 84.

92. Emily Hahn, *Times and Places* (New York: Thomas Y. Crowell Company,

1937), 96–102.

93. Ibid., 102.

94. See Appendix B and Appendix C.

95. Weigle and Babcock, *Great Southwest*, 47. The authors do not include the actual numbers of patrons from 1926 or 1927.

96. See Appendix B and Appendix C. Many of the AT&SF records were lost in the 1940s because of a fire at the Topeka office, per phone conversation with KSHS archivist Connie Menninger, November 6, 2000.

97. "What do you know about the Forgotten Peoples of Puyé and Ci-cu-yé of Pueblo Bonito and Penasco Blanco-of Aztec and Mesa Verde?" *National Geographic Magazine* (June 1928), 768.

98. "The Indian-detour," *National Geographic Magazine* (January 1929), 144.

99. Marta Weigle "From Desert to Disney World: The Santa Fe Railway and the Fred Harvey Company Display the Indian Southwest," *Journal of Anthropological Research* 45, No. 1 (Spring 1989), 115–16.

100. Hahn, *Times and Places*, 101.

101. *Indian-detour* (1926), 3–6, MNM. From 1926 into the 1930s the *Indian-detour* brochures gave detailed information on tours, times, and locations.

102. Mather, *Colonial Frontiers*, 99.

103. Thomas, *Southwestern Indian Detours*, 244–45; the 1929 brochure includes a picture of a Packard on its cover. *Indian-detour* (1929), 1, MNM; the 1931 brochure includes pictures of the new Cadillacs. *Indian-detour* (1931), 1, 16, CSWR.

104. "Harvey Makes Announcement of Transfer," *Santa Fe New Mexican*, March 16, 1931, No. 64, p. 1, col. 8, MNM.

105. Ibid.

106. Unfortunately, comparable statistics are not available for previous decades.

107. Rothman, *Devil's Bargains*, 143–45, 162, 165.

108. See Appendix A.

109. See Appendix B.

110. See Appendix C.

111. *New Mexico: A Guide to the Colorful State* (New York: Hastings House, 1940; reprinted as *The WPA Guide to 1930s New Mexico* (Tucson: University of Arizona Press, 1989), 188.

112. Weigle, "From Desert to Disney World," 115.

113. Ibid.

114. *La Fonda in Old Santa Fé* (Chicago: Rand McNally, 1929), 4, MNM, VF "Hotels."

115. Mather, *Colonial Frontiers*, 98; Weigle "From Desert to Disney World," 115.

116. Quoted in Mather, *Colonial Frontiers*, 98.

117. Armitage, *Operation Santa Fe*, 154; Dilworth, *Imagining Indians*, 131; Duke, Fred Harvey, 380; Weigle and Babcock, *Great Southwest*, 81, 161, 163.

118. Dilworth, *Imagining Indians*, 129; Howard and Pardue, *Inventing the Southwest*, 124–125; McLuhan, *Dream Tracks*, 45; Weigle and Babcock, *Great Southwest*, 67–70. The Santa Fe and the Harvey Company were "recognizable force[s] in the development of the Indian market nationally," in Mather, *Colonial Frontiers*, 98.

119. *White Metal Universe: Navajo Silver from the Fred Harvey Collection* (Phoenix: The Heard Museum, 1981), 7.

120. Dexter Carillo, *Southwestern Indian Jewelry* (New York: Abbeville Press, 1992), 68;

Weigle and Babcock, *Great Southwest*, 161–62; Dilworth, *Imagining Indians*, 132.

121.   Armitage, *Operation Santa Fe*, 154; Dilworth, *Imagining Indians*, 82–83, 131–41; McLuhan, *Dream Tracks*, 44.

122.   Letter to H. Schweizer from J. F. Huckel (July 18, 1932), HM, RC39 (1): 9. "Indian Design" jewelry was produced by American workmen on "silver blanks, on which the Indian designs are hand stamped, are cut out from silver plate with a die and the setting that hold the Turquoise are stamped out by machinery," in a memorandum called "Statement of Facts, Regarding Indian Design Coin Silver Jewelry Manufactured by the H. H. Tammen Company, Denver Colorado" (July 21, 1933); letter to J. F. Huckel From H. Schweizer (September 29, 1932), HM, RC39 (1): 9.

123.   Letter to H. Schweizer from F. Clough (September 15, 1931); Letter to J. F. Huckel from H. Schweizer (September 17, 1931), HM, RC39 (1): 9; Weigle and Babcock, *Great Southwest*, 60–63.

124.   Ibid.

125.   Dilworth, *Imagining Indians*, 132.

126.   Letter to J. F. Huckel from H. Schweizer (September 17, 1931), HM, RC39 (1): 9.

127.   Hahn, *Times and Places*, 104.

128.   Letter to J. H. McMillan at the Spanish-Indian Trading Company in Santa Fe from H. Schweizer (September 18, 1931). The owner of the H. H. Tammen Company, who had been producing dye-stamped silver "Indian Design Jewelry," fought the bill. But in 1933 the company compromised by attaching labels of authenticity to its jewelry and crafts; in letter to H. Schweizer from Carl Lichtenberg at the H. H. Tammen Company (July 20, 1933); "Statement of Facts," from the H. H. Tammen Company (July 21, 1933), regarding their "Indian 'Design' Jewelry... produced by American workmen," letters from HM, RC39 (1): 9.

129.   Letter to J. F. Huckel From H. Schweizer (September 29, 1932), HM, RC39 (1): 9.

130.   See Appendix C.

131.   Ibid.

132.   Some of the writers include Sandra D'Emelio, Leah Dilworth, Kathleen Howard, Diana Pardue, and Marta Weigle.

133.   Dilworth, *Imagining Indians*, 82.

134.   McLuhan, *Dream Tracks*, 45.

135.   Dilworth, *Imagining Indians*, 77–124; Weigle and Babcock, *Great Southwest*, 207.

136.   Dilworth, *Imagining Indians*, 49; Weigle and Babcock, *Great Southwest*, 161. The array of Santa Fe brochures promoting the town of Santa Fe produced from 1915 to 1940 include photographs and illustrations of Pueblos, Hopis, and Navajos, but exclude any representation of the Apache people.

137.   McLuhan, *Dream Tracks*, 45; Weigle and Babcock, *Great Southwest*, 161–62.

138.   Dilworth, *Imagining Indians*, 101; Weigle, "From Desert to Disney World," 115.

139.   Ibid.

140.   The stories included A. J. A. Duganne, "The Peon or the Yankee Knight Errant," in *Beadle's Dime Novels* (New York: Beadle and Company, 1861); and Major Sam Hall, "The Serpent of El Paso," *Beadle's Dime Library* (New York: Beadle and Adams, 1882).

141.   *Old Santa Fe and Roundabout* (The Atchison, Topeka and Santa Fe Railway Co, 1923), 3.

142.   *Indian-detour* (1926), 5–6, MNM Harveycars Motor Cruises, *Off the Beaten Path in the Great Southwest* (1928), 13–14, MNM.

143.   See Appendix C.

144.   Ibid.

145.   *WPA Guide to 1930s New Mexico*, 165.

146.   Elizabeth Kay, *Chimayó Valley Traditions* (Santa Fe: Ancient City Press, 1987), 14.

147.   Helen Lucero and Suzanne Baizerman, *Chimayó Weaving: The Transformation of Tradition* (Albuquerque: University of New Mexico Press, 1999), xviii.

148.   *WPA Guide to 1930s New Mexico*, 295.

149.   Ibid.

150.   Lucero and Baizerman, *Chimayó Weaving*, xviii; Marta Weigle, ed., *Hispanic Villages of Northern New Mexico* (Santa Fe: Lightning Tree, 1975; repr. of Tewa Basin Study, v. 2, *Hispanic Villages of Northern New Mexico*, Santa Fe: Jene Lyon, Publisher, 1935), 86.

151.   Ibid., xix.

152.   These weavings are available at the Basket Shop in Old Town Plaza in Albuquerque and at Ortega's de Chimayó in Chimayó, a short drive from Santa Fe.

Chapter Four

1.   See Appendix A for a list of *Indian-detours* brochures.

2.   Weigle and White, *Lore of New Mexico*, 417.

3.   Rothman, *Devil's Bargains*, 84.

4.   Ibid., 84–96, 98–102.

5.   W. H. Simpson to E. L. Hewett, May 15, 1913; E. L. Hewett to W. H. Simpson, June 9 1913, MNM, Hewett Collection, AC105. Hewett was hired to mastermind the building of the New Mexico State Building and assist with the Santa Fé Railway Indian Exhibit, "Painted Dessert," at the Panama-California Exposition of 1915 in San Diego.

6.   "Remarkable Program to be Given at the Santa Fe Fiesta," *The Santa Fe Magazine* (August 1920), 45.

7.   "Paul A. F. Walter, "The Santa Fe Fiesta: Marvelous Pageant Depicting the History of New Mexico to be held again," *The Santa Fe Magazine* (September 1920), 27.

8.   Ibid., 28.

9.   Ibid.

10.   Ibid.

11.   Ibid., 29.

12.   Charles E. Parks, "City of Santa Fe Reenacts Stirring Deeds of the Conquistadores," *The Santa Fe Magazine* (November 1920), 21.

13.   Ibid., 22.

14.   Ibid., 26–27.

15.   Walter, "Santa Fe Fiesta," 27; Rothman, "Devil's Bargains," 102–4. Hewett invited dancers from several Pueblos to showcase local culture and for the edification of visitors.

16.   Photograph caption, "A Bunch of Old-timers in the Santa Fe, N.M., Fiesta Parade," *The Santa Fe Magazine* (March 1923), 30.

17.   *The Fiesta of Santa Fe* (Santa Fe: Santa Fe New Mexican, 1924), 4. All Santa Fe Fiesta programs were collected from MNM, Vertical Files, "Santa Fe Fiesta."

18.   Ibid., back cover.

19.   The word *Zozobra* in Spanish means "worry," "anxiety."

20.   Weigle and White, *Lore of New Mexico*, 417.

21.   Ibid., 418; Wilson, *Myth of Santa Fe*, 213.

22.   Charles F. Lummis "The Capital of Our Romance," *Official Santa Fe Fiesta Program* (1929), 24.

23.   *Official Santa Fe Fiesta Program* (1929), 36.

24.   Leona Browne. "Re-discovery of Old Santa Fe," *The Santa Fe Magazine* (October 1926), 40.

25.   Ibid., 42.

26.   Wilson, "Myth of Santa Fe," 206.

27.   Ibid.

28.   *The Santa Fe Magazine* (August 1920), 45; (September 1920), 27–29; (November 1920), 21–32; (March 1923), 30; October 1926), 40–42.

29.   "Receipts from Donators for 1930," MNM, Santa Fe Fiesta, Box 201, M72–6/7.

30.   *Santa Fe Fiesta* (Chicago: Passenger Traffic Santa Fe Systems Lines, 1935), 2.

31.   L. J. Cassel. "Ancient City of Santa Fe Celebrates: This Year's Fiesta—the 227th—One of Brilliance and Gaiety," *The Santa Fe Magazine* (October 1939), 7–11.

32.   Ibid., 7.

33.   Ibid., 10.

34.   *Santa Fe: The Official Year 2000 Visitors Guide* (Albuquerque: Starlight Publishing, 1999), 17.

35.   *Old-New Santa Fe* (1912), 2, MNM.

36.   "Development of the Santa Fe Style," *The Santa Fe Magazine* (June 1915), 26–31.

37.   Wilson, *Myth of Santa Fe*, 36.

38.   Ibid., 26.

39.   Rosemary Nusbaum, *The City Different and the Palace* (Santa Fe: Sunshine Press, 1978), 9.

40.   *Old and New Santa Fe and Roundabout* (1916), 6, CSRRM, KSHS.

41.   Bainbridge Bunting, *Early Architecture in New Mexico* (Albuquerque: University of New Mexico Press, 1976), 4; *Old and New Santa Fe and Roundabout* (1916), 7. This brochure claims that Santa Fe's "quaint mission churches [are] far older and better preserved than those of southern California"; *Old and New Santa Fe and Roundabout* (1923), 29, mentions that San Miguel was built in 1636; *Harveycars Motor Cruises: Off the Beaten Path in the Great Southwest* (1928), 42. All information for the citation was gathered at the CSRRM.

42.   Wilson, *Myth of Santa Fe*, 36.

43.   Landt Dennis, *Behind Adobe Walls: The Hidden Homes and Gardens of Santa Fe and Taos* (San Francisco: Chronicle Books, 1997).

44.   Ibid., 45.

45.   Quoted in Simmons, *New Mexico*, 98; Ralph Emerson Twitchell, *Old Santa Fe: The Story of New Mexico's Ancient Capital* (Santa Fe: Santa Fe New Mexican Publication Co., 1925), 168.

46. Wilson, *Myth of Santa Fe*, 44.

47. Ibid., 69.

48. *Old and New Santa Fe and Roundabout* (1916), 13; *Santa Fe: The Gateway of the "Greatest Fifty Mile Square in America"* (Santa Fe: The Santa Fe New Mexican, 1918), 43, MNM; *A Tour of Historic Santa Fe* (Santa Fe: The Santa Fe New Mexican Publishing Co., 1923), 3, MNM.

49. *Santa Fe: The Gateway of the "Greatest Fifty Mile Square in America,"* 43; *Old-New Santa Fe and Roundabout* (1916), 13.

50. Bunting, *Early Architecture in New Mexico,* 109–12; Sheppard, *Creator of the Santa Fe Style*, 5.

51. Wilson, *Myth of Santa Fe*, 99–101.

52. Examples are featured in *Old and New Santa Fe and Roundabout* (1916), 13; *Santa Fe: The Gateway of the "Greatest Fifty Mile Square in America"* (Santa Fe: The Santa Fe New Mexican, 1918), 43, MNM; *A Tour of Historic Santa Fe* (Santa Fe: The Santa Fe New Mexican Publishing Co., 1923), 3, MNM.

53. C. A. Higgins, *To California Over the Santa Fe Trail* (Chicago: Passenger Department, Santa Fe, 1917), 41, KSHA, Box No. 883.

54. *Old Santa Fé and Roundabout* (1923), 27–29, KSHS. The date of occupancy for the Old House differs from brochure to brochure. In *To California Over the Santa Fe Trail,* Higgins claims that Coronado stayed there in 1540.

55. Ibid. A *garita* is a sentry box or lookout tower.

56. *The Indian-detour* (1925), 2–3, MNM.

57. *Roads to Yesterday* (1927), 71, MNM.

58. For descriptions on Santa Fe and its architecture in *The Santa Fe Magazine,* see the following issues: October 1909, 67–74; July 1914, 68; June 1915, 26; May 1916, 25–31; June 1920, 21–26; October 1921, 15–24; October 1926, 40; July 1928, 22–24; February 1929, 23–25; January 9–12, February 1932, 24–26; January 1933, 29–32; April 17–23, November 1935, 43–44; October 1939, 7–11, KSHS.

59. Elizabeth E. Bell, "Old Santa Fe," *The Santa Fe Magazine* (January 1932), 9, KSHS.

60. Ibid., 9.

61. Ibid., 10.

62. "Chile" is the name of the pods and the plant; "chili" is the name of powder and a bowl of the fiery food, defined in Ronald Johnson, *Southwestern Cooking New and Old* (Albuquerque: University of New Mexico Press, 1985), 1.

63. "What's hot?" Santa Fe, Official Visitors Guide, 2000, 82.

64. An excellent book on the history and production of chile in New Mexico is by Carmella Padilla, *The Chile Chronicles: Tales of a New Mexico Harvest* (Santa Fe: Museum of New Mexico Press, 1997).

65. *1921 Business Directory*, 105–10.

66. Erna Fergusson, *Mexican Cookbook* (Santa Fe: Rydal Press, 1934), Fergusson's book includes some recipes that deviate from the traditional foods; for example, one instruction includes macaroni, some recipes contain Worcestershire Sauce, and one dish is served with French dressing; Cheryl Foote, "Southwestern Regional Cookery" (lecture for "A Taste of America: American Food and Foodways Since 1492," history class taught in the spring of 1999), Albuquerque Technical Vocational Institute, Albuquerque.

67. Margarita C.de Baca, *New Mexico Dishes* (N.p., 1937); Foote, "Southwestern Regional Cookery."

68. Cleofas M. Jaramillo, *The Genuine New Mexico Tasty Recipes* (Santa Fe: Seton Village Press, 1942).

69. Fabiola Cabeza de Baca Gilbert, *Historic Cookery* (N.p., 1939; repr., Las Vegas, NM: La Galeria de los Artesanos, 1970); Gilbert, *The Good Life. New Mexico Traditions and Food* (Santa Fe: San Vincenta Foundation, 1949).

70. Foote, "Southwestern Regional Cookery." *Poncha* is a type of cinnamon biscuit, *chicos* are dried sweet corn kernels that are soaked in water before they are eaten or blended into other foods, and *atol* is a hot corn gruel.

71. *La Fonda* (1929).

72. Ibid.

73. *La Fonda* (circa 1930), back cover.

74. *La Fonda Menu* (N.p., 1951); La Fonda Menu (N.p., 1954), SWRC.

75. *La Fonda Menu* (N.p., 1954).

76. *To Travel and Ticket Agents—Fred Harvey Hotels and Hotel Restaurants* (Chicago: Fred Harvey, February 1956). In New Mexico: Santa Fe, Albuquerque.

77. *Harvey Girls' Recipes* (Albuquerque: Vinegar Tom Press, 1971), 9, 11. This book contains recipes from the wives of Santa Fe Railroad workers and Harvey House chefs from 1910 to 1913.

78. *Santa Fe Visitors Guide 2000*, 83–84. Thirty-two out of seventy-seven cafés and restaurants within walking distance of the Plaza offer New Mexican or Southwestern cuisine.

79. For additional traditional New Mexico cuisine cookbooks, see: Adela Amador, *Recipes From the Family of Adela Amador* (Albuquerque: Amador Publishers, 1991); Ana Baca, *Bueno: The Seasons—A Cookbook for Life* (Albuquerque: El Encanto, 1992); *Cocinas de New Mexico* (Albuquerque: Public Service Company of New Mexico, 1979); William Hardwick, *Authentic Indian-Mexican Recipes* (Tucson: Booksmith, 1965); Jim Martin, *Southwestern Cuisine* (Cortez, CO: Crow Canyon Archaeological Center, 1993); Yolanda Ortiz y Pino *Original Native New Mexican Cooking* (Santa Fe: Sunstone Press, 1993); Millie Santillanes, ed., *New Mexico Feasts* (Albuquerque: Plaza Vieja Publishing, n.d., circa 1993).

Chapter Five

1. Erna Fergusson, *Albuquerque* (Albuquerque: Merle Armitage Editions, 1947), 13; John W. Reps, *Cities of the American West: A History of Frontier Urban Planning* (Princeton: Princeton University Press, 1979), 48.

2. Bradford Luckingham, *The Urban Southwest: A Profile History of Albuquerque—El Paso, Phoenix—Tucson* (El Paso: Texas Western Press, 1982), 22; Marc Simmons, *Albuquerque* (Albuquerque: University of New Mexico Press, 1982), 116.

3. Simmons, *Albuquerque*, 133–34.

4. See Appendix D: Population trends for Albuquerque and Santa Fe.

5. Simmons, *Albuquerque*, 327.

6. C. M. Chase, *The Editor's Run In New Mexico and Colorado* (Montpelier: Argus and Patriot Steambook and Job Printing House, 1882).

7. *WPA Guide to 1930s New Mexico*, 176.

8. Myrick, *New Mexico's Railroads*, 236.
9. Victor Westphall, *History of Albuquerque, 1870–1880* (Master's thesis, University of New Mexico, 1947), 78.
10. John W. Reps, *Cities of the American West: A History of Frontier Urban Planning* (New Jersey: Princeton University Press, 1979), 618.
11. Lina Fergusson Browne, ed., *Trader on the Santa Fe Trail: The Memoirs of Franz Huning* (Albuquerque: University of New Mexico, 1973), 102
12. Reps, *Cities of the American West*, 621.
13. Tobias and Woodhouse, *Santa Fe*, 25.
14. Simmons, *Albuquerque*, 231; Fergusson, *Albuquerque*, 19.
15. Simmons, *Albuquerque*, 231; Fergusson, *Albuquerque*, 20.
16. Anne V. Poore and John Montgomery, eds., *Secrets of a City: Papers on Albuquerque Area Archaeology* (Santa Fe: Ancient City Press, 1987), 58.
17. Sheppard, *Creator of the Santa Fe Style*, 111–15. Some of the buildings in Santa Fe under Rapp's commission include Catron High School—1904; N. B. Laughlin Building—1905; First Ward School—1905; Santa Fe County Jail—1906; St. Vincent Sanatorium/Marian Hall—1908; Executive Mansion—1908; plans for the Masonic Temple—1909, County Courthouse—1910; Elks Club—1911; First National Bank—1911, Gross, Kelly and Co. Warehouse—1914; Sunmount Sanatorium No. 1—1914; Museum of New Mexico—1916; New Mexico Asylum for the Deaf and Dumb—1917; Santa Fe La Fonda—1920.
18. Luckingham, *Urban Southwest*, 35.
19. *Fifteenth Census of the United States* (Washington, D.C.: U.S. Government Printing Office, 1921), 1:151, 730.
20. Ibid. See Appendix D; Tobias and Woodhouse, *Santa Fe*, 26.
21. Luckingham, *Urban Southwest*, 32, 35.
22. Simmons, *Albuquerque*, 287.
23. D. Rogers Daniels, *The Impact of the Santa Fe Railroad on the Albuquerque Area* (compiled for Architecture 562, School of Architecture and Planning, University of New Mexico: 1985), 13.
24. *New Mexico* (Chicago: Poole Bros., 1910), 5, KSHS, GL 385 At2, pam.v.8.
25. Ibid., 30.
26. *The New Mexico Business Directory for 1909–1910*, 877–80.
27. Ibid., 851, 852.
28. Daniels, *Impact of the Santa Fe Railroad*, 13; Lynn, *Windows of the Past*, 13.
29. Lynn, *Windows of the Past*, 17.
30. Ibid., 20.
31. Ibid., 23; Simmons, *Albuquerque*, 373.
32. Lynn, *Windows of the Past*, 45, 46.
33. Koshare Tours was purchased by the Atchison, Topeka, and Santa Fe and renamed Indian Detours. Erna Fergusson, the owner of Koshare Tours, was bought aboard to run the new tour escort service.
34. *Old-New Santa Fe and Roundabout* (1924), 31.
35. *off the beaten path in the Great Southwest* (1928), 18. CSWR, MSS 115 (Southwest Travel Literature), box 1, folder 11.
36. Fred Harvey, ed., *Enchantarama of Albuquerque: 1706–1956* (Albuquerque: Albuquerque Chamber of Commerce, 1956). MNM, AC 333, Box 1, Folder 28.

37. *Along the Route* (Chicago: Rand McNally, April 1958), 12. CSWR, MSS 115 (Southwest Travel Literature), box 1, folder 13.
38. Ibid.
39. *New Mexico Health Resorts*, 12.
40. *Resorts on the Santa Fe* (Passenger Department of the Santa Fe Route, July 1898), 15, 16, 21, 22.
41. Spidel, *Doctors of Medicine*, 88.
42. Tobias and Woodhouse, *Santa Fe*, 61.
43. Ibid., 33. In 1902 there were 166 physicians for the population of 206,000 New Mexicans; ten years later 429 physicians served an estimated population of 350,000.
44. Luckingham, *Urban Southwest*, 58; Simmons, *Albuquerque*, 344.
45. Spidel, *Doctors of Medicine*, 101.
46. Ibid., 146.
47. Tobias and Woodhouse, *Santa Fe*, 59.
48. Luckingham, *Urban Southwest*, 58.
49. Ibid.; Spidle, *Doctors of Medicine*, 87.
50. *New Mexico State Business Directory 1950* (Albuquerque: University of New Mexico Printing Plant, 1950), 124–28; *Santa Fe City Directory 1953* (El Paso: Hudspeth Directory Co., 1953), 502, 508.
51. See Appendix E.
52. Lacking cash, Navajo and Pueblo clients often secured credit at trading posts by pawning turquoise and silver jewelry in order to purchase livestock and other necessities for their livelihoods. When livestock was sold, the debt at the trading post would be paid. If the debt was not paid within the specified period set by the client and the trader, the pawnbroker could then "re-sale" the item.
53. Tobias and Woodhouse, *Santa Fe*, 189.
54. Daniels, *Impact of the Santa Fe Railroad*, 14; Jessica Dixon, *Architecture of the Santa Fe Railroad* (Albuquerque: Historic Preservation, 1986), 8, Albuquerque Planning Library, HE2791 S36 D59; *Southwest Railroad Notes* (November 1996), 3, CSWR, Vertical Files, Railroads—AT&SF.
55. Mary Kay Cline, interview by the author, July 9, 2003, notes, Albuquerque Convention and Visitors Bureau, Albuquerque, NM.
56. Appendix G. Lodgers' tax is widely used to determine tourism statistics. Unfortunately there is no distinction between business and leisure patrons using the area's accommodations.
57. Appendix G; New Mexico Department of Tourism: Travel Statistics. *Lodger's Tax* (August 1, 2003), hhttp://newmexico.org/Industry/lodgerstax.html.
58. Marc Simmons, interview by the author, July 15, 2003, notes, Los Cerrillos, NM.
59. Ibid.

Chapter Six

1. *Santa Fe Visitors Guide 2000*, 13–19. This slogan was printed on a city brochure in the early 1920s. *The City Different: Descriptive Guide to Santa Fe and Vicinity* (Santa Fe: Chamber of Commerce, n.d.), MNM, Santa Fe Guide Books.
2. *Old Santa Fe and Roundabout* (1923), 6, KSHS.
3. Dilworth, *Imagining Indians*, 5.

4. Ibid.
5. "Santa Fe Developed Advertising Art," *The Santa Fe Magazine* (March 1923), 45–46.
6. *Indian-detour* (1929), 61–62; *Indian-detour* (1930), 35, 41, 63, NMSRA.
7. Howard and Pardue, *Inventing the Southwest*, 95–97; Weigle and Babcock, *Great Southwest*, 3–4, 149–50.
8. *Harveycars Motor Cruises: Off the Beaten Path in the Great Southwest* (1928), 12, MNM.
9. "Spanish-Indian," *Santa Fe: Dude Ranch Country* (Chicago: R. H. Donnelley Deeptone and Sons Co., 1935).
10. Some books by Charles Lummis include *Letters From the Southwest; New Mexico David; Land of Poco Tiempo* (New York, 1893; repr., Albuquerque: University of New Mexico Press, 1952); and *Mesa, Cañon, and Pueblo* (New York: The Century Press, 1925). Some books by Zane Grey include *Captives of the Desert* (New York: W. J. Black, 1926); and *Fighting Caravans*. New York: Grosset and Dunlap, 1929).
11. These authors included Adolf Bandelier, Erna Fergusson, Oliver LaFarge, Mabel Dodge Luhan, and Mary Austin, among others.
12. Weigle and Babcock, *Great Southwest*, 62–63; Howard and Pardue, *Inventing the Southwest*, 93–95.
13. Richard Bradford, *Red Sky at Morning* (Philadelphia: J. B. Lippincott Company, 1968); Jo-Ann Mapson, *Blue Rodeo* (New York: HarperCollins, 1994); and John Nichols, *The Milagro Beanfield War* (New York: Holt, Rinehart and Winston, 1974).
14. Roger W. Birdseye, "The Indian Detour," *The Santa Fe Magazine* (April 1926), 45.
15. *Santa Fe Visitors Guide 2000*, 14–15.
16. Ibid.
17. *Santa Fe Visitors Guide*, 13.
18. Sheppard, *Creator of the Santa Fe Style*, 102.
19. *Condé Nast Traveler* (November 1999), 231; *Condé Nast Traveler* (November 2000), 247.
20. http://www.concierge.com/cntraveler/lists/readerschoice02/topcities; http://www.travelandleisure.com/worldsbest/pressrelease-ny.cfm.

Bibliography

PRIMARY SOURCES
I. Directories/Guide and Promotional Books and Materials

A. California State Library: California History Section (CSL)

Business Directory of New Mexico and Gazetteer of the Territory. Santa Fe: New Mexico Printing and Publishing Co, 1882.

Census of Population. Washington, DC: U.S. Government Printing Office, 1880; 1890; 1900; 1910; 1920; 1930; 1940; 1999; 2000.

Pointers on the Southwest. Topeka: Sexton Printer, 1883. Microfilmed in "Western Americana: Frontier History of the Trans-Mississippi West, 1550–1900." New Haven: Research Publications, 1975.

Santa Fe. New York: Sanborn Map Company, 1882; 1886; 1890; 1898; 1902; 1908; 1913; 1921; 1930.

B. California State Railroad Museum Library (CSRRM)

Off the Beaten Path in New Mexico and Arizona. For Atchison, Topeka and Santa Fe Railway Co., Chicago: Rand McNally & Co., 1921.

Old-New Santa Fe and the Roundabout. Chicago: Press of the Henry O. Shepard Co., 1916.

Old-New Santa Fe and the Roundabout. Chicago: Hedstrom-Barry Co., 1923.

C. Heard Museum, Phoenix, AZ (HMA)

Black, W. J. *The Indian Detours: Newest Way to see Oldest America.* Chicago: Norman-Monroe, 1926.

———. *They Know New Mexico: Intimate Sketches by Western Writers.* N.p.: Passenger Department of the AT & SFRW, 1928.

Dorsey, George A. *Indians of the Southwest.* Chicago: Passenger Department of the AT & SFRW, 1903. (Distribution 15,000)

The Great Southwest Along the Santa Fe. Kansas City: Fred Harvey Co., 1921.

Harveycar Motor Cruises off the beaten path into the Great Southwest. N.p.: Rand McNally & Co., 1928.

Post Card Collection

Roads to Yesterday Along Indian-detours. N.p.: Fred Harvey, n.d.

Santa Fe, New Mexico and Vicinity, ca. 1926.

D. Kansas State Historical Society, Topeka, KS (KSHS)

Agriculture and Horticulture. Santa Fe: New Mexico Printing Co., 1898.

Climatology and Mineral Spring of New Mexico—Health and Pleasure Resorts. Santa Fe: New Mexico Printing Company, 1900. Photos by and courtesy of The Santa Fe Route.

Free Lands and Dry Farming in the Southwest. Chicago: Blakely-Oswald Printing Co., 1910.

Higgins, C. A. *To California Over the Santa Fe Trail.* Chicago: Passenger Department, Santa Fe, 1917.

Ho! To the Land of Sunshine: A Guide to New Mexico for the Homeseeker. Albuquerque: New Mexico Bureau of Immigration, 1909.

New Mexico. Chicago: Poole Bros., 1910.

New Mexico Health Resorts. Topeka: Passenger Department of the AT & SF RW, 1897.

New Mexico: A Land of Prosperity and Happiness. Chicago: Rand, McNally & Co., 1891.

The New Southwest: New Mexico Rio Grande Valley, Arizona Salt River Valley. Chicago: Rand, McNally & Co., circa 1895.
Old-New Santa Fe and Roundabout. Chicago: Press of the Henry O. Shepard Co., 1916.
Old-New Santa Fe and Roundabout. Chicago: Hedstrom-Barry Co., Printers, 1923.
Resorts on the Santa Fe. Passenger Department, Santa Fe Route, 1898.
Santa Fe All the Way. Chicago: The Henry O. Shepard Co., 1907.

E.   Museum of New Mexico, Fray Angélico Chávez History Library, Santa Fe, NM (MNM)
A Tour of Historic Santa Fe. Santa Fe: The Santa Fe New Mexican Publishing Co., 1923.
Climate is Fate—New Mexico. Santa Fe: New Mexico Printing Co., 1900.
Colorado, New Mexico, Utah, Nevada, Wyoming and Arizona Gazetteer and Business Directory 1884–5. Vol. 1. Chicago: R. L. Polk and Co. and A. C. Danser, 1884.
Grey, Zane. "An Appreciation of New Mexico." *Santa Fe: The Gateway of the "Greatest Fifty Mile Square in America."* Santa Fe: The Santa Fe New Mexican, 1918.
Harveycars Motor Cruises off the beaten path in the Great Southwest. Chicago: Rand McNally & Co., October 1928.
Harveycar Motor Cruises off the beaten path in the Great Southwest. Chicago: Rand McNally & Co., 1929.
The Indian-detour. Chicago: Rand McNally & Co., 1925.
Indian-detour. Topeka: Atchison, Topeka and Santa Fe Railway Co., 1926.
"La Fonda," At the End of the Trail. N.p., 1921.
La Fonda in Old Santa Fé: The Inn at The End of the Trail. Rand McNally & Co., 1929.
La Fonda: Santa Fe, New Mexico. Kansas City: Alco-Geavure, 1936.
McKenney's Business Directory1882–1883. San Francisco: Pacific Press, 1882.
Meany, Rev. Edward Willcocks. *Santa Fe, Health Resort.* Santa Fe: New Mexican Printing Company, 1890.
New Mexico: The Sunshine State. Chicago: Henry O. Shepard Co., 1913.
New Mexico: The Sunshine State. Chicago: Henry O. Shepard Co., 1917.
Nicholson, Ceo. T. *New Mexico.* Topeka: Gen. Passenger and Ticket Agent A.T. & S.F. R.R., n.d. (flyer).
Off the Beaten Path in New Mexico and Arizona. Chicago: Press of the Henry O. Shepard Co., 1917.
Old-New Santa Fe and the Roundabout. Topeka: Atchison, Topeka and Santa Fe Railway Co., 1912.
Old-New Santa Fe and the Roundabout. Chicago: Hedstrom-Barry Co., Printers, 1924.
Old Santa Fe and Vicinity: Points of Interest and Convenient Trips. Historical Society of New Mexico. Santa Fe: El Palacio Press, 1930.
Pacific Coast Directory for 1888–9: Business Directory of San Francisco, Central and Southern California, Arizona, New Mexico and Southern Colorado. San Francisco: McKenney Directory Co., 1888.
Places of Interest in Santa Fe, New Mexico. Presidential edition, 1903.
Roads to Yesterday: Motor Drives Out from Old Santa Fé. Chicago: Hedstrom-Barry Co., Printers, 1927.
Santa Fe: The Gateway of the "Greatest Fifty Mile Square in America." Santa Fe: Santa Fe New Mexican, 1918.
Santa Fe Fiesta. Chicago: Passenger Traffic, Santa Fe System Lines, 1935.
Santa Fe Fiesta, Official Program. Santa Fe: Santa Fe New Mexican Publishing Corporation, 1924, 1925, 1926, and 1929.
Santa Fe, New Mexico: The Ancient City. Santa Fe: Santa Fe Chamber of Commerce, 1929.
Sights of Santa Fe. The New Mexican Printing Co., 1910.
Steele, Rose W. "Yesterday and Today in Santa Fe." *The Great Southwest Magazine.*

BIBLIOGRAPHY

The Atchison, Topeka and Santa Fe Railway Co., July 1908.

F. New Mexico State Records and Archives, Santa Fe, NM (NMSRA)
Indian Detours—Most Distinctive Motor Cruise Service in the World. Chicago: Rand McNally, 1930.
New Mexico Business Directory. Denver: The Gazetteer Publishing Co., 1909–1910; 1913–1914; 1920; 1921; 1930.
"1998/99 Santa Fe Area Wide, NM." *Polk City Directory.* Livonia: Polk City Directory, 1998.
Resources of New Mexico. Santa Fe: New Mexico Book and Job Printing Department, 1881.
Ritch, William G. *Illustrated New Mexico.* Santa Fe: New Mexican Printing and Publishing, 1883.
Santa Fe City Directory. El Paso: Hudspeth Directory Company, 1930–1931; 1932–1933;1936–37; 1940.
"2000 Santa Fe, NM." *Polk City Directory.* Livonia: Polk City Directory, 1999.

G. University of New Mexico, Center for Southwest Research, Albuquerque, NM (CSWR)
Courier Cars. Chicago: Santa Fe System Lines, 1932.
daily Xcursions. Chicago: Rand McNally & Company, 1925.
Indian-detours: off the beaten path in the Great Southwest. Chicago: Rand McNally, 1931.
Indian-Detours, Roundabout Old Santa Fe New Mexico. Chicago: Rand McNally, 1940.
La Fonda Menu. N.p., 1951; 1954.
Santa Fe: Dude Ranch Country. Chicago: R. H. Donnelley Deeptone and Sons Co., 1935.

II. Manuscripts and Collections
A. Heard Museum and Archives (HM)
Fred Harvey Art Collection Exhibition of 1976
Fred Harvey Company Ephemera Collection
Native American Post Card Collection
Travelogue.

B. Museum of New Mexico, Fray Angélico Chávez History Library (MNM)
Hewett Collection

C. New Mexico State Records and Archives, Santa Fe, NM (NMSRA)
Adellia Collier Collection
R. Hunter Clarkson Collection
Konopek Files
N. B. Laughlin Papers
Shuler-Berninghaus Files

III. Newspapers and Magazines
A. California State Library: California History Section (CSL)
Land of Sunshine. Los Angeles: F.A. Pattee and Co., October 1896; January 1898; November 1898; April 1899; June 1900; December 1901.

B. Museum of New Mexico, Fray Angélico Chávez History Library (MNM)
Daily New Mexican. March 1881.
Weekly New Mexican. 19 July 1879; 14 February 1880; 4 April 1880.
The Santa Fe Magazine. November 1908; December 1920.
Santa Fe New Mexican. February, March 1922; May 1926; September 1927; March 1931.

Santa Fe Republican. June 1848.

C.   Heard Museum (HMA)
McClure's. September 1899; February 1912.
The Nation. November 1921.

D.   Kansas State Historical Society (KSHS)
The Earth. January 1905; January 1906; July 1907.
The Santa Fe Magazine. October, November 1907; November 1908; March, May, July,
        August, September, October 1909; March, May, June, July, August 1912; July 1913;
        June, July, November 1914; March, June 1915; May 1916; June, September 1919;
        May, June, August, September, November, December 1920; May, August,
        October 1921; February, March 1922; March 1923; September 1924; April, October
        1925; April, October 1926; July 1928; January, February, June, July 1929; January,
        February 1932; January, September 1933; April, November 1935; October 1939.

E.   State of New Mexico State Records and Archives, Santa Fe, NM (NMSRA)
Albuquerque Morning Journal. August 1925; May 1926.
New Mexico Magazine. June 1995.
Observer. March 1930.

F.   University of California, Davis, Special Collections, and Shields Library (UCD)
National Geographic Magazine. June 1928; January 1929.
Out West. V. 29, September 1908; V. 6, October 1913.

G.   University of New Mexico, Center for Southwest Research, Albuquerque, NM
        (CSWR).
The Philadelphia Inquirer. March 1926; March 1927.
Westphall, Victor. *History of Albuquerque, 18701880.* Master's thesis, University of New
        Mexico, 1947.

IV. Published Primary Sources

Austin, Mary. *The Land of Little Rain.* Boston: Houghton Mifflin and Co., 1903.
———. *The Land of Journeys' Ending.* New York: The Century Co., 1924.
———. *Starry Adventure.* Boston: Houghton Mifflin Co., 1931.
Bandelier, Adolph, F. *The Delight Makers.* New York: Dodd, Mead and Co., 1890.
Berger, John A. *Fernand Lungren.* Santa Barbara: Schaur Press, 1936.
C. de Baca, Margarita. *New Mexico Dishes.* N.p., 1937.
Calvin, Ross. *Sky Determines.* Albuquerque: MacMillan Company, 1934. Reprint,
        Silver City: High-Lonesome Books, 1993.
Carrington, M.D., Paul M. *The Climate of New Mexico, Natures Sanatorium for
        Consumptives.* Fort Stanton: AR Elliott Publishing Co., 1907.
Chase, C. M. *The Editor's Run In New Mexico and Colorado.* Montpelier: Argus and
        Patriot Steambook and Job Printing House, 1882.
———. *Our Southwest.* New York: Alfred A. Knopf, 1940.
Duganne, A. J. A. "The Peon or the Yankee Knight Errant." *Beadle's Dime Novels.*
        New York: Beadle and Company, 1861.
Fergusson, Erna. *Dancing Gods.* New York: Alfred A. Knopf, 1931.
———. *Mexican Cookbook.* Santa Fe: Rydal Press, 1934.
Gilbert, Fabiola Cabeza de Baca, *Historic Cookery.* N.p., 1939. Reprint, Las Vegas,
        NM: La Galeria de los Artesanos, 1970.
Gregg, Josiah. *The Commerce of the Prairies.* Edited by Milo Milton Quaife. New

York: Citadel Press, 1968.

Grey, Zane. *Captives of the Desert*. New York: W. J. Black, 1926.

———. *Fighting Caravans*. New York: Grosset and Dunlap, 1929.

Hahn, Emily. *Times and Places*. New York: Thomas Y. Crowell Company, 1937.

Hall, Major Sam. "The Serpent of El Paso." *Beadle's Dime Library*. New York: Beadle and Adams, 1882.

Harper's. V. 8, No. 47, April 1854.

Harvey, Fred. *The Great Southwest: Along the Santa Fe*. Kansas City: Fred Harvey, 1914.

Henderson, Alice Corbin. *Modern Indian Painting*. New York: The Exposition of Indian Tribal Arts, 1931.

———. *Red Earth: Poems of New Mexico*. Chicago: R. F. Seymour, 1920.

Holling, Clancy. *New Mexico Made Easy*. Chicago: Rockwell F. Clancy Co., 1923.

Horgan, Paul. *Main Line West*. New York: Harper and Brothers Publishers, 1936.

James, Bushrod W. A. M., M.D. *American Resorts with Notes Upon Their Climate*. Philadelphia: F. A. Davis, 1889.

James, George Wharton. *New Mexico: The Land of the Delight Makers*. Boston: The Page Company, 1920.

La Farge, Oliver. *Laughing Boy*. Boston: Houghton Mifflin Company, 1929.

Lummis, Charles. *Letters From the Southwest: September 20, 1884, to March 14, 1885*. Edited by James W. Byrkit. Tucson: The University of Arizona Press, 1989.

———. *A New Mexico David and Other Stories and Sketches of the Southwest*. New York: Scribner and Sons, 1905.

———. *Land of Poco Tiempo*. New York, 1893. Reprint, Albuquerque: University of New Mexico Press, 1952.

———. *Mesa, Cañon, and Pueblo*. New York: The Century Press, 1925.

Lummis, Charles, ed. *Land of Sunshine: The Magazine for California and the West*. Los Angeles: Land of Sunshine Publishing Company, 1895.

The Official 2000 Santa Fe Visitors Guide. Albuquerque: Starlight Publishing, 1999.

Otero, Miguel A. *Report of the Governor of New Mexico to the Secretary of the Interior, 1903*. Washington, D.C.: Government Printing Office, 1903.

Poore, Anne V., and John Montgomery, eds. *Secrets of a City: Papers on Albuquerque Area Archaeology*. Santa Fe: Ancient City Press, 1987.

Sabin, Edwin. *The Rose of Santa Fé*. Philadelphia: George W. Jacobs and Co., 1923.

Smalley, Eugene V. *History of the Northern Pacific Railroad*. New York: G. P. Putnams's Sons, 1883.

Steinbeck, John. *Tortilla Flat*. New York: The Modern Library, 1937.

Twitchell, Ralph Emerson. *The Leading Facts of New Mexico's History*. Cedar Rapids: The Torch Press, 1912.

———. *Old Santa Fe: The Story of New Mexico's Ancient Capital*. Santa Fe: Santa Fe New Mexican Publication Co., 1925.

Walter, Paul A. "The Santa Fe-Taos Art Movement," *Art and Archeology* 4 (December 1916).

SECONDARY SOURCES
V. Published and Unpublished Secondary Sources

Adams, Samuel Hopkins. *The Harvey Girls*. Cleveland; World Publishing Company, 1942.

Armitage, Merle. *Operation Santa Fe*. Edited by Edwin Corle, New York: Duell, Sloan and Pearce, 1948.

Armstrong, Ruth. *Enchanted Trails*. Santa Fe: New Mexico Magazine, 1980.

Baca, Elmo. *Mabel's Santa Fe and Taos: Bohemian Legends, 1900–1950*. Salt Lake City: Gibbs-Smith, 2000.

Baur, John E. *Health Seekers of Southern California, 1870–1900.* San Marino: The
 Henry E. Huntington Library and Art Gallery, 1959.
Beachum, Larry. *William Becknell: Father of the Santa Fe Trade.* El Paso: Texas Western
 Press, 1982.
Beebe, Lucius, and Charles Clegg. *Rio Grande: Mainline of the Rockies.* Berkeley:
 Howell-North Books, 1962.
Beck, Warren A. *New Mexico: A History of Four Centuries.* Norman: Oklahoma
 Press, 1962.
Berger, John A. *Fernand Lungren.* Santa Barbara: Schauer Press, 1936.
Bradley, Glen Danford. *The Story of Santa Fe.* Boston: The Gorham Press, 1920.
Browne, Lina Fergusson. ed. *Trader on the Santa Fe Trail, The Memoirs of Franz
 Huning.* Albuquerque: University of New Mexico, 1973.
Bryant, Keith L. *History of Atchison, Topeka, and Santa Fe Railway.* New York:
 Macmillan, 1974.
Bunting, Bainbridge. *Early Architecture in New Mexico.* Albuquerque: University of
 New Mexico Press, 1976.
Carillo, Dexter. *Southwestern Indian Jewelry.* New York: Abbeville Press, 1992.
Cavalier, Julian. *Classic American Railroad Stations.* San Diego: A. S. Barnes and
 Co., 1980.
Coan, Charles F. *A History of New Mexico.* Chicago: The American Historical
 Society, 1925.
Coke, Van Dern. *Taos and Santa Fe: The Artists' Environment.* Albuquerque: University
 of New Mexico Press, 1963.
Crandall, Elizabeth. *Santa Fe.* Chicago: Rand McNally and Company, 1965.
Daniels, D. Rogers. *The Impact of the Santa Fe Railroad on the Albuquerque Area.*
 Compiled for Architecture 562, School of Architecture and Planning,
 University of New Mexico, 1985.
Davis, William Watt Hart. *El Gringo or New Mexico and Her People.* Santa Fe: Rydal
 Press, 1938.
Decker, Leslie E. *Railroads, Lands, and Politics.* Providence: Brown University, 1964.
Deloria, Philip. *Playing Indian.* New Haven: Yale University Press, 1998.
D'Emelio, Sandra, and Susan Campbell. *Visions and Visionaries: The Art and Artists of
 the Santa Fe Railway.* Salt Lake City: Peregrine Smith Books, 1991.
Dennis, Landt. *Behind Adobe Walls: The Hidden Homes and Gardens of Santa Fe and
 Taos.* San Francisco: Chronicle Books, 1997.
Dilworth, Leah. *Imagining Indians in the Southwest: Persistent Visions of a Primitive
 Past.* Washington, D.C.: Smithsonian Press, 1996.
Dispenza, Joseph. *Will Shuster: A Santa Fe Legend.* Santa Fe: Museum of New Mexico
 Press, 1989.
Donnelly, Thomas C. *The Government of New Mexico.* Albuquerque: The University
 of New Mexico Press, 1947.
Duke, Donald. *Santa Fe: The Railroad Gateway to the American West.* Vol. 2. San
 Marino: Golden Books, 1995.
———. *Fred Harvey, Civilizer of the American Southwest.* Acada: Pregel Press, 1995.
Dutton, Bertha P. *Indians of the Southwest.* Englewood Cliffs, NJ: Prentice-Hall, 1975.
Eldredge, Charles C., Julie Schimmel, and William H. Truettner. *Art in New Mexico,
 1900–1945, Paths to Taos and Santa Fe.* New York: Abbeville Press, 1986.
Eliot, Jane. *The History of the Western Railroads.* New York: Exeter Books, 1985.
Fergusson, Erna. *Albuquerque.* Albuquerque: Merle Armitage Editions, 1947.
———. *New Mexico: A Pageant of Three Peoples.* New York: Alfred A. Knopf , 1951.
———. *Our Southwest.* New York: Knopf, 1940.
Foote, Cheryl. "Southwestern Regional Cookery." Lecture for "A Taste of America:

BIBLIOGRAPHY

American Food and Foodways Since 1492," history class taught at Albuquerque: Albuquerque Technical Vocational Institute, spring 1999.

Fox, Steven D. "Healing, Imagination, and New Mexico." *New Mexico Historical Review* 58 (July 1983).

Garber, Susan. *The Feast of Santa Fe: Cooking of the American Southwest.* New York: Simon and Schuster, 1985.

———. *The Good Life, New Mexico Traditions and Food.* Santa Fe: San Vicenta Foundation, 1949.

Gerhard, Peter. *The Northern Frontier of New Spain.* Norman: University of Oklahoma Press, 1993.

Gibson, Arrell Morgan. *The Santa Fe and Taos Colonies: Age of the Muses, 1900–1942.* Norman: University of Oklahoma Press, 1983.

Grattan, Virginia L. *Mary Colter: Builder Upon Red Earth.* Flagstaff: Northland Press, 1980.

Greever, William S. *Arid Domain: The Santa Fe Railway and Its Western Land Grant.* Stanford: Stanford University Press, 1954.

Gurley, Fred. *New Mexico and the Santa Fe Railroad.* San Francisco: The Newcomen Society in North America, 1950.

Gutiérrez, Ramón A. *When Jesus Came, the Corn Mothers Went Away.* Stanford: Stanford University Press, 1991.

Harvey Girls' Recipes. Albuquerque: Vinegar Tom Press, 1971.

Henderson, James David. *Meals by Fred Harvey: A Phenomenon of the American West.* Fort Worth: Texas Christian University Press, 1969.

Hertzog, Peter. *La Fonda: The Inn of Santa Fe.* Portales: Bishop Printing and Litho. Co., 1962.

Higgins, C. A., *To California Over the Santa Fe Trail,* Chicago: Passenger Department, Santa Fe, 1917.

Horgan, Paul. *The Centuries of Santa Fe.* New York: E. P. Dutton and Co., 1965.

———. *Great River: The Rio Grande in North American History.* 2 vols. New York: Ribehart and Co., 1954.

Horn, Calvin. *New Mexico's Troubled Years.* Albuquerque: Horn and Wallace Publishers, 1963.

Howard, Kathleen L., and Diana F. Pardue. *Inventing the Southwest: The Fred Harvey Company and Native American Art.* Flagstaff: Northland Publishing, 1996.

Hungerford, Edward. "A Study in Consistent Railroad Advertising," *The Santa Fe Magazine.* March 1923.

Jaramillo, Cleofas M. *The Genuine New Mexico Tasty Recipes.* Santa Fe: Seton Village Press, 1942.

Johnson, Byron A., and Robert K. Dauner. *Early Albuquerque: A Photographic History 1870–1918.* Albuquerque: The Albuquerque Journal and The Albuquerque Museum, 1981.

Johnson, Ronald. *Southwestern Cooking New and Old.* Albuquerque: University of New Mexico Press, 1985.

Jones, Billy M. *Health-Seekers in the Southwest, 1817–1900.* Norman: University of Oklahoma Press, 1967.

Kay, Elizabeth. *Chimayó Valley Traditions.* Santa Fe: Ancient City Press, 1987.

Knaut, Andrew L. *The Pueblo Revolt of 1680: Conquest and Resistance in Seventeenth-Century New Mexico.* Norman: University of Oklahoma Press, 1995.

La Farge, Oliver. *Santa Fe: The Autobiography of a Southwestern Town.* Norman: University of Oklahoma Press, 1959.

Lamar, Howard R. *The Far Southwest, 1846–1912: A Territorial History.* Albuquerque: University of New Mexico Press, 2000.

Lecompte, Janet. *Rebellion in Rio Arriba 1837*. Albuquerque: University of New Mexico, 1985.

Limerick, Patricia Nelson. "Seeing and Being Seen: Tourism in the American West." In *Over the Edge: Remapping of the American West*, edited by Valerie J. Matsumoto and Blake Allmendinger. Berkeley: University of California Press, 1999.

Lucero, Helen, and Suzanne Baizerman. *Chimayó Weaving: The Transformation of Tradition*. Albuquerque: University of New Mexico Press, 1999.

Luckingham, Bradford. *The Urban Southwest: A Profile History of Albuquerque—El Paso, Phoenix—Tucson*. El Paso: Texas Western Press, 1982.

Lynn, Sandra D. *Windows of the Past: Historical Lodging of New Mexico*. Albuquerque: University of New Mexico Press, 1999.

McLuhan, T. C. *Dream Tracks: The Railroad and the American Indian 1890–1930*. New York: Harry N. Abrams, Publishers, 1985.

Marshall, James. *Santa Fe, the Railroad That Built an Empire*. New York: Random House, 1945.

Mather, Christine, ed. *Colonial Frontiers: Art and Life in Spanish New Mexico, The Fred Harvey Collection*. Santa Fe: Ancient City Press, 1983.

Mercer, Lloyd J. *Railroads and Land Grant Policy: A Study in Government Intervention*. New York: Academic Press, 1982.

Meyer, Michael C., and William L. Sherman. *The Course of Mexican History*. 5th ed. New York: Oxford University Press, 1995.

Mickelson, Sig. *The Northern Pacific Railroad and the Selling of the West: A Nineteenth-century Public Relations Venture*. Sioux Falls: Center for Western Studies, 1993.

Moody, John. *The Railroad Builders*. New Haven: Yale University Press, 1919.

Moorhead, Max L. *New Mexico's Royal Road: Trade and Travel on the Chihuahua Trail*. Norman: University of Oklahoma Press, 1958.

Morris, Juddi. *The Harvey Girls: the Women Who Civilized the West*. New York: Walker and Co., 1994.

Myrick, David F. *New Mexico's Railroads*. 2d ed. Albuquerque: University of New Mexico Press, 1990.

Noble, David Grant, ed. *Santa Fe: History of an Ancient City*. Santa Fe: School of American Research Press, 1989.

Novak, Barbara. *Nature and Culture: American Landscapes and Painting, 1825–1875*. New York: Oxford University Press, 1980.

Nusbaum, Rosemary. *The City Different and the Palace*. Santa Fe: Sunshine Press. 1978.

The Official 2000 Santa Fe Visitors Guide. Albuquerque: Starlight Publishing, 1999.

Padilla, Carmella. *The Chile Chronicles: Tales of a New Mexico Harvest*. Santa Fe: Museum of New Mexico Press, 1997.

Palmer, Gabrielle G. *El Camino Real de Tierrra Adentro*. Santa Fe: New Mexico Bureau of Land Management, No. 11, 1963.

Poling-Kemps, Lesley. *The Harvey Girls: Women Who Opened the West*. New York: Paragon House, 1989.

———. *Far From Home: West by Rail with the Harvey Girls*. Lubbock: Texas Tech University Press, 1994.

Pomeroy, Earl. *In Search of the Golden West: The Tourist in Western America*. New York: Alfred A. Knopf, 1957.

Potter, Kanet Greenstein. *Great American Railroad Stations*. New York: Preservation Press, 1996.

Powell, Lawrence Clark. *Southwest Classics: The Creative Literature of the Arid Lands, Essays on the Books and their Writers*. Los Angeles: The Ward Ritchie Press, 1974.

Preston, Douglas. "The Granddaddy of the Nation's Trail Began in Mexico." *Smithsonian* 26, No. 8 (November 1995).

BIBLIOGRAPHY

Price, V. B. *Albuquerque: A City at the End of the World.* Albuquerque: University of New Mexico Press, 1992.

Reeve, Frank D. *History of New Mexico.* New York: Lewis Historical Publishing Company, 1961.

Reeve, Kay Aiken. "Santa Fe and Taos 1898–1942: An American Cultural Center." *Southwestern Studies* 67 (El Paso: Texas Western Press, 1982).

Repp, Stan. *The Super Chief. . . Train of the Stars.* San Marino: Golden West Books, 1980.

Reps, John W. *Cities of the American West: A History of Frontier Urban Planning.* Princeton: Princeton University Press, 1979.

Roberts, Calvin A., and Susan A. Roberts. *New Mexico.* Albuquerque: University of New Mexico Press, 1988.

Robertson, Edna, and Sarah Nester. *Artists of the Canyons and Caminos: Santa Fe, the Early Years.* N.p., 1976.

Robinson, Cecil. *With the Ears of Strangers: The Mexican in American Literature.* Tucson: University of Arizona Press, 1963.

Rothman, Hal K. *Devil's Bargains: Tourism in the Twentieth-Century American West.* Lawrence: University Press of Kansas, 1998.

Sarber, Mary A. *Charles F. Lummis: A Bibliography.* Tucson: University of Arizona, 1977.

Sando, Joe S. *Pueblo Nations: Eight Centuries of Pueblo History.* Santa Fe: Clear Light Publishers, 1992.

———. *Pueblo Profiles.* Santa Fe: Clear Light Publishers, 1998.

Sheppard, Carl D. *Creator of the Santa Fe Style: Isaac Hamilton Rapp, Architect.* Albuquerque: University of New Mexico Press, 1988.

Sherman, John. *Santa Fe—A Pictorial History.* Santa Fe: William Gannon, 1983.

Simmons, Marc. *Albuquerque.* Albuquerque: University of New Mexico Press, 1982.

———. *The Last Conquistador: Juan de Oñate and the Settlement of the Far Southwest.* Norman: University of Oklahoma Press, 1991.

———. *New Mexico: a Bicentennial History.* New York: W. W. Norton and Company, 1977.

———. "Santa Fe in the Days of the Trail." In *Santa Fe: History of an Ancient City*, edited by David Grant Noble. Santa Fe: School of American Research Press, 1989.

———. *Yesterday in Santa Fe.* Cerrillos, NM: San Marcos Press, 1969.

Smith, F. B. *The Retreat of Tuberculosis 1850–1950.* London: Croom Helm, 1988.

Spidel, Jake W., Jr. *Doctors of Medicine in New Mexico.* Albuquerque: The University of New Mexico Press, 1986.

Thomas, Diane H. *The Southwestern Indian Detours: The Story of the Fred Harvey/Santa Fe Railway Experiment in 'detourism.'* Phoenix: Hunter Publishing Co., 1978.

Tobias, Henry J., and Charles E. Woodhouse. *Santa Fe, A Modern History, 1880–1990.* Albuquerque: University of New Mexico Press, 2001.

Twitchell, Ralph Emerson. *The Conquest of Santa Fe, 1846.* Edited by Bill Tate. Truchas: Tate Gallery, 1967.

Udall, Sharyn Rohlfsen. *Modernist Painting in New Mexico, 1913–1935.* Albuquerque: University of New Mexico Press, 1984.

———. *Santa Fe Art Colony, 1900–1942*: July 17–August 8, 1987, Gerald Peters Gallery, Santa Fe, New Mexico. Santa Fe: Gerald Peters Gallery, 1987.

Velásquez, Rita C., ed. *Directory of American Scholars.* V. 1, 9th ed. Detroit: The Gale Group, 1998.

Villani, John. "Artists Took Ride on the Santa Fe." *New Mexico Magazine* 69, No. 11 (November 1991).

Waklsman, Selman A. *The Conquest of Tuberculosis.* Berkeley: University of California Press, 1964.

Waters, L. L. *Steel Trails of Santa Fe.* Lawrence: University of Kansas Press, 1950.

Weber, David J. *New Spain's Far Northern Frontier.* Dallas: Southern Methodist University Press, 1979.

Weigle, Marta. "Exposition and Mediation: Mary Colter, Erna Fergusson, and the Santa Fe/Harvey Popularization of the Native Southwest, 1902–1940," 117–50. *Frontiers* 12, No. 3 (Niwot: University of Colorado Press, 1992).

———. "From Desert to Disney World: The Santa Fe Railway and the Fred Harvey Company Display the Indian Southwest. " *Journal of Anthropological Research* 45, No. 1 (Spring 1989).

Weigle, Marta, ed. *Hispanic Villages of Northern New Mexico.* Santa Fe: Lightning Tree, 1975. Reprint of Tewa Basin Study, V. 2, *Hispanic Villages of Northern New Mexico.* Santa Fe: Jene Lyon, Publisher, 1935.

Weigle, Marta, and Peter White. *The Lore of New Mexico.* Albuquerque: University of New Mexico Press, 1988.

Weigle, Marta, and Kyle Fiore. *Santa Fe and Taos: The Writer's Era, 1916–1941.* Santa Fe: Ancient City Press, 1982.

Weigle, Marta, and Barbara A. Babcock, eds. *The Great Southwest of the Fred Harvey Company and the Santa Fe Railroad.* Phoenix: The Heard Museum, 1996.

White Metal Universe: Navajo Silver From the Fred Harvey Collection. Phoenix: The Heard Museum, 1981.

Wilson, Chris. *The Myth of Santa Fe: Creating a Modern Regional Tradition.* Albuquerque: University of New Mexico Press, 1997.

Worley, E. D. *Iron Horses of the Santa Fe Trail.* Dallas: Southwest Railroad Historical Society, 1965.

The WPA Guide to 1930s New Mexico. Tucson: The University of Arizona Press, 1989.

Zeleny, Carolyn. *Relations Between the Spanish-Americans and the Anglo-Americans in New Mexico.* Arno Press: New York, 1974.

Index

INDEX

INDEX